'ON THE FRONTLINE' LEARNING SERIES

The
Teenage Parent's
Child Support Guide

Barry T. Schnell

This book is an excellent consumer resource for teenage parents and all teenagers. It is an indispensable resource tool for teachers, librarians, counselors, child support advocates, and social service providers.

PUBLISHER'S NOTE

This publication is designed to provide accurate and authoritative information in regard to the subject matter covered. It is sold with the understanding that the publisher is not engaged in rendering legal or other professional services. If expert assistance or legal counsel is needed, the services of a competent professional should be sought. The opinions and conclusions expressed are solely those of the author and do not necessarily represent the views of any governmental or private agency.

Copyright © 1988 by The Advocacy Center for Child Support, Inc.

All rights reserved. No part of this book may be reproduced, stored in a retrieval system, or transmitted in any form or by any means electronic, mechanical, photocopying, recording, or otherwise without express written permission of the author or publisher, except for brief quotations in critical reviews.

Acknowledgments for illustrations:
We thank the Georgia Office of Child Support Recovery for permission to reprint their tabloid flier "Looking Beyond Teenage Pregnancy". For information about the program or flier, contact the Office of Child Support Recovery, Georgia Department of Human Resources, Room 529, 878 Peachtree Street N.E., Atlanta, Georgia 30309.

We are also indebted to Ms. Susan Moore, Ms. Deb Larimore, and The Marion County Child Support Division of Indianapolis, Indiana, for permission to reproduce "Teenage Parents: Choices & Responsibilities."

We would like to express our sincere thanks to the Texas Attorney General's Office for permission to reprint the flier "Teenage Parents: Child Support Rights and Responsibilities."

We also thank the National Institute for Child Support Enforcement for permission to reprint illustrations contained in *History and Fundamentals of Child Support Enforcement*. The cartoons were designed by Bruce H. Bollinger and Linda Willard.

A special thanks to the National Institute of Mental Health for permission to reproduce the illustrations in their pamphlet "Learning While Growing: Cognitive Development".

Library of Congress Catalog Card Number: 88 081534

ISBN: 0910599-26-2

Published by The Advocacy Center for Child Support, Inc.

Printed in the United States of America

Contents

ACKNOWLEDGMENTS............................VIII

CHAPTER I
CHOICES AND REALITIES 10
    Introduction 10
    Young Unwed Mothers............................ 13
    Young Unwed Fathers 17
    Guidelines for Becoming a Father 19

CHAPTER II
RESOURCE DIRECTORY FOR TEENS 24
    Other Places To Turn 26
    Emergency Assistance 26
    Child Care.. 27
    Hospital and Adolescent Parenting Programs 29

CHAPTER III
PATERNITY SERVICES............................ 31
    Blood Testing..................................... 32
    Do You Need a Lawyer? 33
    Why Unwed Mothers May Not Pursue Paternity .. 34
    Why Unwed Fathers May Not Admit Paternity ... 36
    Benefits of Paternity 38
    Signing the Birth Certificate 40
    Paternity Interview with the Mother.............. 41
    Texas Attorney General's Office - Flier 43
    Teenage Parent's: Choices & Responsibilities 45

CHAPTER IV
SUPPORT IN THE FAMILY COURTS 53
    Understanding Roles in Child Support
    Enforcement 55
    What is the Family Court? 57
    Child Support and Public Assistance 59
    Preparing Your Case 59
    Child Support Information Checklist.............. 60

    Going to Court 61
    Order of Protection 63
    Custody and Visitation 64
    Importance of Legal Custody 64
    How Do I Get Visitation?......................... 65
    Understanding Your Court Order 65
    Enforcing Your Court Order 65
    Grandparent's Responsibility 66
    Looking Beyond Teenage Pregnancy 67

CHAPTER V
TEEN PARENTS AND WELFARE 71
    Problems Teen Parents Have in Applying for
    Social Services................................... 73
    Application Process for Welfare 75
    Family Welfare Reform Act....................... 76
    The AFDC Check 77
    Grant Amount 77
    Your First Welfare Interview 78
    Application Steps 79
    What is Meant by "Cooperation"? 80
    How and When to Claim Good Cause 82
    Caution! 83
    Tips For Dealing with Social Service Agencies.... 84
    Young Fathers and Welfare 85
    Work Requirements and Welfare 85
    College Students and Welfare 86

CHAPTER VI
FOOD STAMPS 88
    Supplemental Food Program for Women,
    Infants, and Children (WIC)..................... 91

CHAPTER VII
MEDICAID AND HEALTH SERVICES 94
    Application Process 96
    What Health Services Are Covered 97

Medi-Cal 98
Child/Teen Health Plan 99
Prenatal Care 99
Homeless Teen Families 101

CHAPTER VIII
THE LAW AND TEEN PARENTS 102
Going to School: If You Have Children or Are
Pregnant, You Have Rights!..................... 105
Teen Parent Curriculum 106
Schools for Pregnant Teens and Teen Parents 107
Legal Assistance Programs and Teen Parents 108
Emancipation Of Minors 109

CHAPTER IX
STAY IN SCHOOL 113
Job Training Helps!.............................. 115
Getting a Job 115
Job Discrimination.............................. 116

CHAPTER X
TEEN PARENTS WHO ARE TAKING
RESPONSIBILITY 118

GLOSSARY 123

EXHIBITS*

I. Sample Blood Test 126
II. Sample Interrogatory Of Alleged Father......... 127

*All exhibits are for illustrative and educational purposes and are not legal documents.

BIBLIOGRAPHY 128

STATE CHILD SUPPORT PROGRAMS 131

INDEX... 135

To my wife, Heather, a bonnie Scottish lass, and to Schuyler, Wesley, and Melissa, my three children.

ABOUT THE AUTHOR

Barry T. Schnell is a former Administrative Analyst for the Child Support Enforcement Program in New Jersey. He is an advocate for teenage parents and a member of the National Organization on Adolescent Pregnancy and Parenting, Inc.

The author was born in Philadelphia, Pennsylvania, in 1944. He attended The Pennsylvania State University and received an M.A. degree from Rider College. He lives in Newark, Delaware, with his wife, Heather.

ACKNOWLEDGMENTS

First we would like to thank the young members of our Teen Parents Advisory Committee for their helpful suggestions in making this book relevant to teen parents. Throughout the development of this book we spoke to over 200 teen parent program directors, family court judges, and child support, health care, and social service providers who have daily contact with young parents.

We are especially indebted to Ms. Deb Larimore, Ms. Susan Moore, and the Marion County Prosecutor's Office of Indianapolis, Indiana for permission to reprint "Teenage Parents: Choices and Responsibilities." Also, Ms. Celia Boswell and the Georgia Department of Human Resources for permission to reprint their tabloid newspaper for teenagers, "Looking Beyond Teenage Pregnancy."

We would also like to thank Dr. Gladys Vaughn of the American Home Economics Association, The Attorney General's Office of Texas, and Mr. John Beckman of The City of New York. Also, Ms. Wendy McNeil of The Teen Outreach Program of The Association of Junior Leagues, Ms. Sharon Rodine of the National Association on Adolescent Pregnancy and Parenting, Inc., Ms. Lillian Tereszkiewicz of the National Center on Youth Law, and Ms. Jeanne Lindsay of Morning Glory Press.

Valuable resource materials were provided by Ms. Charlene Clemens of the Family Service Agency of San Francisco and also The Children's Defense Fund. The Pregnancy Networks in New York City were quite helpful. A special thanks to Nancy Nunez of the Bronx Teenage Pregnancy Network.

A special thanks to Esther Wattenberg of the University of Minnesota and Mercer Sullivan of the Vera Institute of Justice for their help and advice.

Ms. Suzanne Bergeron of the National Urban League was quite helpful, as were the Mayor's offices of Chicago and New York City. We really appreciate all the cooperation we received from the following organizations: Brooklyn Legal Services Corporation; Family Life Information Exchange; Ford Foundation; Healthy Mothers, Healthy Babies Coalition; March of Dimes Birth Defects Foundation; and the SHARE Resource Center on Teen Pregnancy Prevention.

Also, we would like to extend our sincere thanks to Reverend Kathy Cooper-Ledesma of the Southern California Interfaith Hunger Coalition for permission to adapt materials from their booklet—*How to Get Food and Money: The People's Guide to Welfare and Other Services in Los Angeles County.* Last, but not least, we would like to thank the Monroe County Legal Assistance Program for permission to adapt information in their fliers.

The entire research process was thoroughly enjoyable. All the hundreds of people we worked with are totally dedicated professionals striving to help teenage parents.

Chapter I

Introduction

As a teenage parent, you need to ask yourself: "What are the best interests of my child?" "What are my needs for survival and growth?" As you make these choices, you are trying to define who you really are. You are struggling to give your life direction, meaning, and dignity.

This chapter will:

- Discuss the needs teen mothers have for themselves and their children.
- Describe the concerns that many young unwed fathers have.

Choices and Realities

All teenage parents and their children have the right to adequate food, clothing, shelter, medical care and other types of assistance. Young parents have the right to complete their education. They have the right to apply for social services in a humane atmosphere of courtesy, consideration, and respect without discrimination on account of race, color, national origin, sex, or marital status. Assistance from social service agencies should be administered to teen parents so as to encourage self-respect and self-reliance.

Although most young people have the desire to be independent and self-supporting, it does not mean you should try to do everything yourself. Teenage parents often need a support network which may include friends, family, religious leaders, teachers, counselors, doctors, social workers, child care, health clinics, legal assistance, and other community resources.

Your support network may change as you face new challenges as a teen parent. A good support network is built on people and organizations you can trust and depend on to really help you with problems and concerns. **With a good support network teen parents can make decisions without having to wait until a problem becomes a crisis.**

Teen parents need medical and nutritional help for themselves and the children. Many young parents need child care services, welfare (Aid to Families with Dependent Children), food stamps, WIC (Women, Infants and Children), and medicaid. Often young unwed parents need counseling to help them continue their education. They need help in learning parenting skills and advice and direction for becoming emotionally secure.

All minor parents need to know how to protect and enforce their rights. They need to know what to do if certain benefits they receive are discontinued, or they are told they don't qualify for certain services. They need to understand their right to a quality education. Teenage parents need to know their rights regarding child support, paternity, custody, visitation, emancipation, and legal assistance.

For many teen parents the change from a high school student with few responsibilities to being a parent is not smooth. Yet being a teen parent can be a rewarding and fulfilling experience. Regardless of how many people may be helping, you are the parent, and no one can replace you. Don't be afraid to ask questions, and don't turn down sincere offers of help.

As a teen parent you cannot afford to dwell on past mistakes. You cannot change the past. You must make decisions that will make your life better—now—for yourself and your family.

YOUNG UNWED MOTHERS

Many teen mothers need access to child support services. They need to understand that the child support office is required to provide a full range of services to teen mothers at little or no cost. These services include locating absent parents, legally naming the father of the child (paternity establishment), making and enforcing support orders and visitation orders, and collecting and distributing child support payments.

It is important for many teen mothers to weigh the pros and cons of paternity establishment—that is, legally naming the father of the child. It is necessary for young unwed mothers to understand the short-term and long-term benefits that flow to her and the child as a result of establishing paternity.

Teenage mothers need to know how to prepare for court and what to do when they are in court. Young unwed mothers go to court for many reasons: establishing paternity, seeking legal custody, enforcing child support rights, seeking emancipation, or having a restraining order made which prevents someone from bothering the mother or the child.

Many young mothers are scared of and intimidated by the courts. This book has helpful information for these teenage parents. It explains the role of the various court officials and how the court can help them.

Many teen parents need to explore their feelings about welfare. They need to understand that welfare is not charity, but a government program provided for individuals with certain needs. **For many teen parents, welfare, food stamps, and medicaid are three bridges over troubled waters. These social services give them a chance to cope and regroup before moving on toward independence.**

Just because a teen parent has a legal right to public assistance (AFDC) does not mean that it is easy to get. Applying for welfare and staying on welfare require a lot of time and effort in filling out forms, collecting documents, and dealing with overburdened welfare workers.

Teen mothers need to know how to protect and enforce their rights when applying for welfare (AFDC), food stamps, WIC (Women, Infants, and Children) and medicaid or Medi-Cal. What is your obligation for naming the father of your child? What are your rights to a fair hearing when your rights have been violated?

Many teen mothers need information about their legal rights. Are the teenage mothers in your neighborhood entitled to free legal assistance? What groups and organizations are available to help teen parents?

Young mothers have many kinds of legal problems. They may need information about emancipation. That is, a minor parent who has become self-supporting, handles her own financial affairs, and sets up her own separate household. Teen mothers need to understand the role of court-appointed guardians. Because you are a minor, a guardian may be appointed to help protect your rights when you have a legal problem. Teen mothers also need to know their legal rights to an education, job training, housing, and health care and child care services.

Most teen parents are unable to expect quick, overnight solutions to many of the problems they are facing. This book is written, however, to get you started in understanding and meeting these concerns. It is written to help teen parents make the best decisions for themselves and their family.

Knowing Your Rights

Young mothers often must be assertive, responsible, and persistent when interacting with social service agencies. **For many teenage parents the bottom line is knowing how to protect and enforce your rights and your child's rights.**

The Teenage Parent's Child Support Guide is dedicated to helping teen parents overcome barriers and get the benefits to which they are entitled by law. There are many reasons why teen parents do not enforce their rights and receive the benefits they need. Many teens receive inaccurate and misleading information about the system. Often teen parents don't have enough information to make the best decisions. They may not know how or where to get this information. Because of emotional stress and fear, many teens are afraid to stand up for their rights.

Some young parents refuse to assert their rights because of a feeling of shame or hurt pride from believing myths about many of these programs. Some teen parents give up out of anger and frustration because they find it so difficult to work with the system. Other teen parents have practical problems of transportation, language, and physical handicaps.

Most teen mothers have a strong desire to become independent and self-supporting. They want to complete their education and find a good job. They want good housing and health care for themselves and their child. They want to feel good about themselves and their futures. The information provided in this book is designed to help teenage mothers achieve these goals.

Teenage mothers have needs:

- Prenatal care for you and the baby. You must take care of yourself. A healthy mother means a healthy baby. Poor nutrition can hurt the mother as well as the baby. Many illegal prescriptions and over-the-counter drugs can cause birth defects. A pregnant woman should not take any drugs unless absolutely necessary—and then only when prescribed by a doctor. Even alcohol can have a serious effect on a fetus.
- Good food for you and the child. Frequent eating at fast-food outlets may result in substandard intakes of iron, calcium, and vitamin A. Good nutrition is essential.
- Reliable and affordable child care.
- Education in a school or teen parent program.
- A support system, which may include friends, relatives, a religious leader, counselors, a doctor, a social worker, teachers, community leaders, and organizations such as the Salvation Army, Red Cross, and YWCA.
- Counseling and opportunities to share feelings with other teenage parents.
- To know your rights when applying for social services such as welfare, medicaid, food stamps, and WIC.
- To know how to protect and enforce your rights regarding child support, paternity, custody, and visitation.
- Parenting classes to help you meet the demands of your child.
- Emergency services such as child abuse hotlines and shelters for homeless teenage parents.
- Job skills and job programs that will help you to become self-supporting.

YOUNG UNWED FATHERS

A young unwed father may not admit to being the father of his child. Some young fathers are afraid of the courts and want to avoid contact with them. Some young fathers are unsure that the child is theirs. Recent studies have shown, however, that many young unwed fathers have informal arrangements to help provide for the mother and child. While they have not admitted paternity "legally," they have acknowledged it in their community.

A study funded by the Ford Foundation indicated that many young fathers were enthusiastic about helping their partner and child. At the end of a two-year program, 82% of the teenage fathers reported having daily contact with their children, 74% said they contributed to the child's financial support, and almost 90% maintained a relationship with the mother.

Never forget, you are the father of your child, and no one can replace you. When you spend time with your child, you are giving much more than financial support. "A real man is a good father." Sure, you may feel a bit uncomfortable in your parenting role. You may have to learn how to feed and change your baby. It's a wonderful feeling to hear your baby's heartbeat, to look at your baby smile as it recognizes you and your voice.

You may ask yourself: "How can I be a good father? I don't have a job or money. I don't have a high school education." It's a big responsibility. Your schedule may be difficult. It may not be easy to continue your education and help with your baby. You may have to put more emphasis on the quality of time you have with your child.

A large number of young unwed fathers want to help nurture their children. They have not abandoned the mother of their child. Even though they may not have much money, they try to be supportive in other ways. They may help with the babysitting, housecleaning, and food shopping.

Young unwed fathers need to know:

- That many counties have special programs for young unwed fathers. Normally the child support unit will not try to force young fathers out of school in order to collect child support. In many counties, the judge will order the young man to pay a minimum amount of support if he feels that the father is capable of making a contribution from a part-time job.

- That if their child is on public assistance, the father is building a debt in the amount of the welfare grant. In some counties, efforts to name the father legally and enforce child support will be postponed until the father is 18 years old or out of school.

- That in some states the amount of debt can be limited by the young father having a court order for child support. For example, while the child is receiving $225 monthly from welfare, the father may have a token court order of only $15 a month. This amount, then, may be your debt to the state. Thus, in some cases a young father may limit his obligation by admitting paternity.

- That in some states if the young unwed father admits to paternity he may be charged with statutory rape. It is a crime to have sexual intercourse with a woman under a certain age (usually 16), even if both parties consent.

- **That until it is legally determined that you are the father of the child, you have no legal visitation rights. If your relationship with the mother falls apart, she can stop you from seeing the baby.** There is some truth to the saying "A woman may become a mother in the hospital, but a man may not become a father." The young unwed father must have his rights legally established by a court in order to enjoy his rights to fatherhood.

- **If you father a child, you must support that child until he or she is 18 years old—no matter how young you are; no matter where you live; no matter what you earn; whether you visit the child or not; whether the mother is on welfare or not—it's the law.**

GUIDELINES FOR BECOMING A FATHER

Health Care

It is important that your partner receives proper medical care. If she doesn't have a doctor, help her find one. Check with friends or community organizations to find out where she can get prenatal care. BE CAREFUL: The mother should not take any drugs—not even aspirin—without permission from her doctor. Remember, if the mother smokes, drinks alcohol, or takes drugs during pregnancy, the baby may suffer. You may encourage her to stop smoking and drinking. Make sure she eats well and gets plenty of rest.

Encouragement and Support

Pregnancy changes a woman physically and emotionally. She may become upset or worried for no apparent reason. Her moods can go up and down. It is important that you be patient and understanding. A little tenderness may help her to feel more relaxed and secure. This will be good for her and the baby.

Father's Moods

As a father-to-be, you may be worried about the future. How can you stay in school? What kind of a father will you be? How can you help the mother? Some expectant fathers even experience signs of pregnancy such as morning sickness. Try to be as helpful as possible. Try to get involved in planning for the baby. Get advice from responsible friends and from groups that work with teen fathers. Help the mother with housework, shopping, or other chores she may have. Go with her on hospital visits.

Many young fathers distrust the courts, schools, and other social service agencies. They really do not understand their rights and responsibilities. They are often unable to make realistic decisions regarding:

- Child support
- Courts
- Custody
- Education
- Emancipation
- Legal assistance
- Paternity
- Social services
- Visitation

Young unwed fathers need to build a strong support network of friends and organizations they can depend on and trust. They need to understand how to protect their rights and become emotionally secure, self-supporting teen parents.

SUMMARY

Many teen parents have trouble gaining access to the legal system because they are minors and have low-incomes. What does a young unwed father do if he is not permitted to see his child? Does a young father in your state have the right to voluntarily admit paternity? Is a young unwed mother legally obligated to name the father of the child when applying for welfare? What are the mother's legal rights to child support and paternity services?

It is important to understand that your children have rights that will be affected by your decisions. As teen parents you need effective and sensitive communications about your rights to social services such as welfare (AFDC), food stamps, medicaid/medi-cal, and WIC. You need public education and outreach services by the courts, schools, and social service agencies. You need to know where to turn for help when you are having problems protecting and enforcing your rights.

As teen parents you have many rights regarding your children. First, you have custody and control of your child. You decide the rules for your family. You choose the child's name and religion. You will be responsible for deciding how your child will be disciplined and educated. Also, you will have to make important decisions about the kind of medical care your child receives.

Yes, teen parents have important rights and responsibilities for their children. We trust that the information presented in this book will help you make sound decisions for you and your family.

This Book Will Help Teen Parents In Many Ways:

- It will motivate you to understand your needs and growth requirements.
- It will help you to build a support network of those individuals, organizations, and community resources that can really help you.
- It will help you to develop responsible decision-making and problem-solving skills based on your personal values and goals.
- It will help you become more assertive, responsible, and persistent in protecting and enforcing your rights and your child's rights.
- It will help you feel more positive about yourself and your future.
- It will help you to manage and improve your life.

Issues for Teen Parents:

- Why are education, child care, and a support network important for teen parents?
- When is it important for teen parents to protect and enforce their rights?
- Regardless of their age, both parents are responsible for the support of their children. What does this mean to you?
- What are several nonfinancial ways that young unwed fathers can support the mother and child?

Chapter II

Getting the system to respond to your needs is an exercise in patience and determination. It is not easy. Remember, you are doing this for your child. You may have to visit several different agencies before you get the answer you're looking for. Don't give up. You will find someone who will be able to help you.

This chapter will:

- Name organizations, groups, and individuals in your community who can help teen parents.
- Describe what is important for an effective child-care program serving parents.
- Explain the role of hospital services for teen parents in your community.

Resource Directory for Teens

There may be many programs and services available in your community to help young parents. These may include community groups, religious organizations, and social services that provide welfare, food stamps, medicaid, and WIC. Also, groups such as legal aid, hospitals, health clinics, and emergency services may exist to help you.

If you have an emergency and are contacting a social service agency, make sure you tell them right away that you have a serious problem. If you are calling from a pay phone, you may want to give the number to the party you are speaking with so that person can call you back if you run out of money. You should try to find out in advance what documents you will need to bring with you. (Never leave original documents with anyone; ask to have photocopies made.) With many programs you will need a social security card and birth certificate.

You will also want to know if there are any costs involved. Find out if you will need permission from your parents to participate in the program. It is also a good idea to learn the hours that the agency is open and if an appointment is required. When you make an appointment, write down the date and time and get good directions for getting there. If you are disabled, you may want to make sure that the location is accessible to you. During the interview you should ask what your rights are and what their policy is regarding confidentiality.

Other Places To Turn

Big Brothers/Big Sisters
Boy's Club/Girl's Club
Boy Scouts/Girl Scouts
Catholic Charities
Child-Care Center
Child Support Office
Church Groups
Counselors
Emergency Services
Family/Clinic Doctor
4H Club
Friends
Health Clinic
Hospital Parenting Program
Legal Services
March of Dimes
Mental Health Center
Minister, Priest, Rabbi
Police/Police Clubs
Red Cross
Salvation Army
Schools
Shelters for Homeless and Battered Persons
State Employment Agency
Teen Parenting Programs
United Way
Urban League
YMCA/YWCA

EMERGENCY ASSISTANCE

You have a right to whatever is necessary to maintain life. This includes food, clothing, shelter, and health care. Many social agencies will deny or delay emergency grants, and you may not know how to deal with this problem. You may need the assistance of a welfare advocate. You may try calling an emergency hotline in your community or calling legal aid for help. Tell them that you have an emergency problem and that you need immediate help. You should also check with the Salvation Army, Catholic Charities, the YM/YWCA, a hospital adolescent parenting program, a shelter for homeless or battered women, or churches and local charities that may provide food and shelter for a few nights.

CHILD CARE

There are an estimated 1.3 million children living with adolescent mothers. There are another 1.6 million children living with mothers who were teens when they were born. Each year approximately half a million teenagers 19 or younger give birth to children. Approximately 50% of the teens who give birth before the age of 18 never complete high school. Remaining in school—a regular school or an alternative high school—is very difficult for many young parents.

In addition to having all the problems that come with being a teenager, you have the special problems of being a mother and having responsibility for a small child. Because many high schools do not offer child-care programs, teenage mothers must often look for infant-care centers in their communities. Most young mothers need help in finding reliable and affordable child care.

Young parents often prefer a family member to watch the baby. Often, however, the grandparents may feel tied down. Also, if either grandparent has to quit or cut back on his or her job to take care of the baby, the whole family may be affected economically and emotionally.

Good child care is healthy for the young mother and her child. It gives you more choices. The teen mother is less isolated and can continue her education with her friends. It reduces many of the pressures of teen parenting and lessens the potential for child abuse. Being a teen parent does not have to be "a one-way ticket to poverty."

Low income teen parents may be able to place their children in free or subsidized day care. Generally you are required to meet certain financial eligibility requirements. Often, even when parents are eligible for publicly funded day care, there may be a long waiting list.

Child-Care Programs

An effective child-care program for young parents should meet the following criteria:

- It should be easy for the teenage parents to get to the child-care center. Round-trip transportation should be provided for parents and children between the school, the child-care center, and the home.

- The center should accommodate young children so that mothers may return to school soon after birth if they choose to do so.

- Its adult-to-child ratio should be within the state guidelines for licensed child-care facilities.

- The children's day should begin shortly before school starts and not end at least until school is dismissed.

- The staff at the center should be trained in early childhood education and have experience working with teenage parents.

- It should not charge a fee if it would prevent parents from using the clinic.

Hospitals and Adolescent Parenting Programs

Many hospitals offer special services to teenagers. When teenagers have their babies in the hospital, social workers visit them, refer them to social services, and encourage them to make well-baby appointments before they leave the hospital.

Other Services Include:

- HEALTH EDUCATION includes prenatal, parenting, and family life/sexuality education for young parents. There also may be support groups for adolescent parents.

- CONTRACEPTION INFORMATION may be provided by an evening adolescent clinic at a nearby medical center.

- HOME HEALTH CARE may include maternal and child health, nursing, monitoring pregnant and parenting teens and their infants, instruction in infant care, and pre- and postnatal education.

SUMMARY

For many teen parents life can be quite difficult. It is important that you know where to turn when you have problems. You should be able to list the people and organizations you can go to for support and assistance such as family members, teachers, friends, clinics, and social services.

If you are having an emergency, make sure you tell them right away. You have a right to adequate food, clothing, shelter, and health care. Call an emergency hotline or legal assistance if you have an urgent problem.

Effective child-care service can help teen parents in many ways. It often gives the young mother more options for staying in school and planning her life. It helps reduce the pressures of teen parenting and lessens the potential for child abuse. **Being a teen parent does not have to be "a one-way ticket to poverty."**

Issues for Teen Parents:

- What programs are available in your community to help teen parents?
- What types of emergency problems do teen parents have, and who can you contact in your community for assistance?

CHAPTER III

When paternity is established, it means that a man is considered the legal father of a child. If a child is born to a married couple, the law presumes that the husband is the father of the child. If a child is born to unmarried parents, a court must declare that the man is the father of the child. Until the court determines the legal father, the man has no visitation or custody rights. Also, the mother cannot get child support from the man until a court decides that he is the father of the child.

This chapter will:

- Describe how blood testing is used by the courts to determine the father of the child.
- Explain several reasons why young unwed mothers may not pursue paternity.
- Explain several reasons why young unwed fathers may not admit paternity.
- Help you understand the benefits of paternity for the child, mother, father, and society.
- Prepare you for a paternity interview with a social worker.
- Describe your rights and responsibilities regarding child support and paternity.

Paternity Services

A paternity case may be filed in a family court. The family court is concerned with the entire family and its legal problems. This court uses counselors, probation officers, psychologists, psychiatrists, and other experts to help meet the needs of families. The case may be filed by the child, the child's mother, or the child's father. Also, the welfare department may file the case if it is likely that the mother or child will need welfare benefits to support themselves.

A paternity case may be filed in court as soon as the mother is pregnant. If the man states that he is not the father of the child, the mother may have to wait until after the child is born before going to court. This is because the court may order blood tests. Blood tests cannot be done until after the baby is born. Usually you have to file the court case before the child reaches the age of 18.

Blood Testing

Blood testing helps to minimize the guesswork involved in determining the father of a child. **Blood tests can show either that the man is definitely *not* the father or that he is *probably* the father, with 99% accuracy.** This is important because a man may be falsely accused of fathering a child (Exhibit I). Blood testing for paternity establishment is based on the scientific principle that individuals inherit traits from their parents. A child inherits genes from his mother and father. Human blood contains many of these genes, and it is possible to use blood tests to identify a father with a high degree of certainty.

There are certain procedures for blood testing. The father, mother, and child may appear at the same time, identify each other, and witness the drawing, labeling, and sealing of the blood specimens. Parents will be required to present identification when they go for a blood test. In addition, your photograph and thumbprint may be taken to record your identity. A footprint may be made of the child.

If the alleged father has signed a written statement that he is the father or has paid child support, the judge will weigh this information when making a decision (Exhibit II). In some states the blood tests are given to all potential fathers. Since a blood test is not final proof of paternity, other evidence is important, including the testimony of the alleged father and testimony of others.

Do You Need a Lawyer?

Admitting paternity is a long-term legal obligation. If someone is trying to prove that you are the father of a child, you may need legal counsel. If you are a minor, you should ask the court to appoint a lawyer for you. You may also want to contact your legal-aid office to see if you qualify for free legal assistance.

The Paternity Trial

The majority of paternity cases are resolved without a trial. There are some cases, however, that require a trial before paternity or nonpaternity can be determined. If an alleged father denies paternity but cannot provide sufficient evidence, he will be named a defendant in a paternity case, and civil proceedings will be undertaken. Generally in a paternity matter it must be determined that the alleged father knew the mother, that he had the opportunity to have sexual intercourse with her, and that the child was conceived during the time frame of their relationship.

Voluntary Acknowledgment of Paternity

Even for the young unwed father who wants to voluntarily, admitting paternity is not that easy. In many counties a guardian or legal counsel must be appointed before a minor can admit paternity. Often it is necessary for the young father to go to court even when he wants to admit paternity. For many young fathers court appearances are intimidating and scary. Having to admit sexual activity before a judge can be difficult. Criminal charges are also a possibility. It is important that young unwed fathers be aware of their rights and responsibilities relating to paternity establishment.

Why Unwed Mothers May Not Pursue Paternity

Some young unwed mothers see paternity as a lost cause. These teens place little emphasis on paternity establishment and child support when the father is young and in school.

They may choose not to pursue paternity for the following reasons:

- They believe that child support is undependable and will provide no immediate benefit.
- They believe that paternity makes no difference if they are receiving welfare.
- They may have had only a passing relationship with the father. Paternity makes it a permanent association.
- They fear that it could ruin their relationship with the father.
- They think that it might upset a relationship with a different male.
- Their parents may be opposed to their trying to establish paternity.
- They see the system—the courts and welfare— as hostile and intimidating.
- They don't enjoy communicating with court officials and caseworkers.
- They have difficulty understanding the procedures and forms.
- They may wish to protect the father from a long-term financial obligation, medical expenses, and possibly jail.
- They see paternity as complicating their life.
- They are afraid of the father.
- They do not know the identity or location of the alleged father.
- They fear losing "off-the-record" payments that the "father" may already be paying.

Why Young Unwed Fathers May Not Acknowledge Paternity

- By acknowledging paternity, the young unwed father may be admitting to a criminal offense. If the woman is under a certain age, he may be guilty of statutory rape—even if she consented.

- The young man may in fact not be the real father. He may have been falsely accused.

- In many states it is quite difficult for a minor to admit paternity. He must have a guardian and/or legal counsel. The states often assign this a very low priority. They will wait until the father is 18 years old or out of school and working.

- The young man is a minor. He does not understand his legal rights. He does not fully understand what admitting paternity involves. He may need legal counsel before admitting paternity.

- Many young fathers view the courts and social service agencies with fear and distrust. They have concerns about going to court and discussing sexual behavior in front of a judge.

- The young father feels he can help his child just as much by "informally" admitting paternity in the community—by helping the mother with "off-the-record" payments and other responsibilities.

- Many young fathers are worried about having to pay child support. They are afraid that they will have to drop out of school to support their child.

- It is in the best interests of the child not to establish paternity when the child was conceived as a result of incest or rape, or if emotional or physical harm to the mother or child could result.

- It is not actively pursued by the child support agency until the father is 18 or employed.

- The mother does not seek paternity or child support services.

- Some young fathers are very immature. They don't understand their legal rights and responsibilities. They don't know where to turn for help. The parents of the young father discourage him from admitting paternity.

- Some young unwed fathers believe that it's not their fault that the girl became pregnant and refuse to accept responsibility.

Both the mother and the father need to weigh carefully the pros and cons of establishing paternity. While the young mother on public assistance may not view child support as important, she should remember that at some future date, when she is no longer receiving public assistance, the payments will be more valuable to her. She should also be aware that she can collect child support payments, up to $50 per month, without affecting her public assistance grant.

The young father must understand that he has few legal rights regarding the child unless paternity is established. He is not entitled to custody and may not be entitled to visitation.

A single mother who applies for public assistance must cooperate with the child support unit by giving information to help determine whether the father can help support the child. The mother is not required to give the father's name if she does not know the name or if she believes—and can prove—that giving the name would threaten her or her child's safety.

A mother, alleged father, or social service agency may bring a paternity action at any time up to the child's 18th birthday.

Benefits of Paternity

- Genetic history: It is in a child's medical interests to know who his or her parents are. Many diseases, illnesses, birth defects, and other conditions are passed to children by their parents. If parents learn of the possibility of passing conditions to their children before they have lost track of them, and are aware that they have parented children in the first place, they may then warn their children of the possible medical disorders.

- The child may be eligible for many short-term and long-term benefits. These include child suppport, social security, disability, veteran's benefits, and inheritance if the parent dies or becomes disabled.

- Paternity can establish an emotional and psychological bond between the parent and child. It is generally in the best interests of children to know their father and have contact with him.

- A young unwed father loves his child. He wants to nurture his child. He wants to "give his child a name." Many children are branded "illegitimate" by society. Having the father may give the child a stronger identity. So-called illegitimate children are often victims of prejudices. When paternity is established, children are not branded this way.

- By admitting paternity, the young father may have his visitation and custody rights legally defined; thus, the mother cannot prevent him from seeing his child.

- If the father joins the armed forces, the child is entitled to many benefits. If paternity is established, the father may receive an extra allowance for the purpose of providing a household for his dependents. This may range from $225 to $340 a month for enlisted men. In addition, the child is eligible for medical care.

- Health insurance: Health care may be available through the father's health care plan.

- All children have a right to be supported to the fullest extent by both parents.

- Establishing paternity helps young parents appreciate the risks and burdens of early parenthood.

- The young father may limit his debt to the state by admitting paternity. The amount of his court-ordered child support may be substantially less than the amount of the welfare grant.

- Establishing paternity may encourage fathers to become more involved in parenting.

- It may be more difficult to establish paternity if it is postponed.

- By acknowledging paternity, the young father shows that he is not trying to avoid his responsibilities and evade the law.

- It is good for society that both parents contribute to their child's well-being.

- A good deal of psychological satisfaction is gained from knowing one's ancestors.

- Paternity provides an opportunity for a sharing of responsibility for the children between the mother and the father.

Signing the Birth Certificate

Young unwed fathers need to understand that in order to be the legal father they must acknowledge paternity. Paternity must be established before the county can require the father to pay child support. Should the young unwed father sign the birth certificate in the hospital? Many young unwed fathers will not sign the certificate at the time of the birth of their child. They are caught up in an emotional experience and may need legal advice and personal counseling before they sign the certificate.

In some cases the young man may not be the father of the child. The entry of an alleged father's name on a birth certificate does not establish paternity in most states. It may serve as evidence, however, for proving paternity.

If the father wants to admit paternity and have his name on the birth certificate but the mother disagrees, the father can have this done with assistance from the courts. Also, if the child carries that father's name on the birth certificate and the mother wishes to change it, the father must be notified and give his approval.

Paternity Interview with the Mother

In the paternity interview, the court will try to establish all the facts regarding the mother's relationship with the alleged father. In the interview, the mother should not be asked questions that have no connection to the pregnancy. Questions that relate to the mother's family or personal history should not be asked. Generally, questions regarding the mother's personal life will be limited to the period during which the child was conceived. The following are possible questions the mother may be asked during a paternity interview:

- When did you begin dating the alleged father? How long?
- Did you ever live with the alleged father? When? How long?
- When did you first have sexual intercourse with the alleged father?
- Did you ever register at a hotel or motel with the alleged father? When? Where?
- Beginning 60 days before you became pregnant, how often did you have sexual intercourse with the alleged father? Where did this take place? Was anyone else present when this took place? Who?

- Did the alleged father use any preventive methods? If so, what?
- What was the date you became pregnant? Why do you believe this date is correct? What was the date of your last menstrual period before this pregnancy?
- When did you tell the alleged father that you were pregnant?
- Did you discuss your pregnancy with the alleged father in the presence of anyone else? Who? When?
- What was the weight of the child at birth?
- Did the alleged father pay any doctor bills?
- Did the alleged father visit you in the hospital?
- Did the alleged father buy anything for the child?
- Did you have sexual intercourse with anyone else other than the alleged father within 45 days prior to or after conception?
- Is there any other information concerning your relationship with the alleged father that you can provide?
- Do you declare under penalty of perjury that this information is true to the best of your knowledge?

In the paternity interview the mother may be advised not to let the father see the baby until he signs the birth certificate and admits paternity. In some cases the mother may be unable to name the father of her child. Also, in some cases the mother may name him but cannot provide evidence to support her claim or information about his whereabouts. (For paternity interview with alleged father, see Exhibit II.)

This flier was developed by the Texas Attorney General's Office. While the paternity laws may be different in your state, it does provide teenage parents with a general understanding of their rights and responsibilities regarding child support and paternity.

PATERNITY

If I was not married to my child's father, is he the legal father? No. He is the *biological father*. Unless certain legal steps are taken after the baby is born, he will not be the child's legal father.

What are the legal steps? Your child's father may voluntarily admit paternity and have an attorney file legal papers with the court which certify that he is the child's father.

What can I do if he refuses to admit that he is the father? You can see an attorney about filing a paternity suit with the court.

What will happen then? The court may order him to give a blood sample which will be used to determine the likelihood that he is the baby's father.

If the court decides he is the father, can my baby have his name? Yes.

If I am pregnant but marry the father before the baby is born, will he be the legal father? Yes.

What can I do to determine paternity and collect support if my baby's father lives in another state? Contact the Attorney General, or a District Attorney, or a County Attorney to find out what needs to be done in your case.

CHILD SUPPORT

Can I collect support from the legal father? If the court rules that he is the child's legal father, the court can order him to pay child support.

Do I have to get a divorce in order to collect child support? No. If you are separated, the court may order your husband to pay child support for his child.

My boyfriend's parents say he cannot be made to pay child support because we were never married. Are they right? No. You can take steps to have him declared the legal father. Once this is done, the court can order him to make child support payments. (see "Paternity")

Can my baby's father be made to pay support if he is only sixteen years old? Yes. If he has an income, he can be ordered to pay support no matter what his age.

If my baby's father is living with his parents and not working, can he still be ordered to pay child support? Yes. Whether he pays support, and if so, how much he pays, depends upon all of his resources, including his ability to work and his personal property.

43

Who decides?	The court makes the final decision about how much he can afford to pay.
If my baby's father refuses to pay support, can I get help from welfare?	You may be able to get Aid to Families with Dependent Children (AFDC), but that depends on your living arrangements.
Will the welfare department make him pay support?	The welfare department—The Texas Department of Human Services—will refer your child's case to the Attorney General of the State of Texas, who will take legal action to determine paternity and collect child support from the father.
If my baby and I are living with my parents, will the baby's father still have to pay child support?	Where you live usually makes no difference whether the court orders the father to pay child support.
If my baby is raised by his father, will I have to pay child support?	Both parents are legally obligated to contribute support even if the child lives with someone other than a parent, such as a grandparent or a foster parent.

FOR THE FATHER

My girlfriend is pregnant and says I am the baby's father. I don't think I am. Can I prove it?	Yes.
How?	First, remember that she must take legal steps to have you declared the father. If she does not do this, then you have no legal obligation.
And what if she files legal papers with the court saying I am the father?	Then you can ask the court to order tests made with blood samples from you, the baby, and the baby's mother.
How accurate are these tests?	There are several tests that can be done with blood samples. Together, they are nearly 100% accurate.
How much child support can I expect to pay?	That depends on how much you earn and what the baby needs. Unfortunately, child support payments hardly ever cover all the costs of rearing a child.
Do I have to pay support if my baby and his mother are on welfare?	Yes. You are required by law to contribute support for your baby. His mother must report your support payments to her welfare worker.

44

TEENAGE PARENTS

CHOICES & RESPONSIBILITIES

"Teenage Parents: Choices & Responsibilities" is an excellent resource for teen parents. It will help you to understand your rights and responsibilities involving paternity, child support, custody, and visitation. It is based on the laws in Indiana. The laws in your state may be different.

TEENAGE PARENTS
CHOICES & RESPONSIBILITIES

"HAVING A BABY WASN'T MY IDEA. I'M NOT READY TO BE A PARENT. I CAN'T HANDLE ALL THESE RESPONSIBILITIES."

"OUR BABY'S HERE, AND I NEED HELP FROM MY BABY'S FATHER!"

"HOW CAN I EVEN BE SURE THAT IT'S MY BABY? I THINK IT IS BUT, I'D LIKE TO BE SURE."

"I KNOW IT'S HIS BABY. HOW CAN I GET HIM TO DO THE THINGS A FATHER SHOULD FOR HIS BABY?"

WHEN A BABY IS BORN TO UNMARRIED PARENTS, THE FATHER HAS NO LEGALLY ENFORCEABLE RIGHTS OR RESPONSIBILITIES AS TO THE BABY.

"PATERNITY MUST BE ESTABLISHED BY A COURT. PATERNITY IS THE PROCESS OF ESTABLISHING A LEGAL FATHER FOR A CHILD BORN OUT OF WEDLOCK."

"MOST PATERNITY CASES ARE VOLUNTARY. THAT IS, THE MOTHER AND THE FATHER BOTH COME FORWARD. IF THE FATHER WON'T COOPERATE, THEN THE MOTHER MUST FILE A LAWSUIT."

HOW CAN I PROVE HE'S THE FATHER?

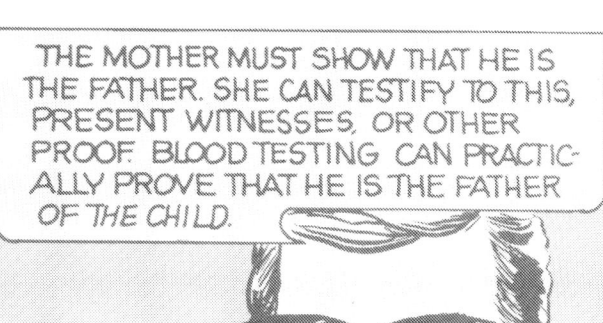

THE MOTHER MUST SHOW THAT HE IS THE FATHER. SHE CAN TESTIFY TO THIS, PRESENT WITNESSES, OR OTHER PROOF. BLOOD TESTING CAN PRACTICALLY PROVE THAT HE IS THE FATHER OF THE CHILD.

WHAT RIGHTS DO I HAVE IN A PATERNITY CASE?

YOU HAVE THE RIGHT TO HAVE AN ATTORNEY REPRESENT YOU, THE RIGHT TO PRESENT YOUR OWN EVIDENCE AND WITNESSES, AND THE RIGHT TO BLOOD TESTING, AMONG OTHERS. A BLOOD TEST CAN SCIENTIFICALLY PROVE YOU ARE NOT THE FATHER OF THE CHILD.

IN SOME CASES, YOU MAY BE ENTITLED TO THE FREE SERVICES OF AN ATTORNEY AND FREE BLOOD TESTING. YOU HAVE AN ABSOLUTE RIGHT TO A JUDGE, OR IN SOME CASES A JURY, TO DECIDE WHETHER YOU ARE THE FATHER.

WHAT HAPPENS IF I AGREE I AM THE FATHER OR THE COURT SAYS THAT I AM AFTER A TRIAL?

THE PROCEDURE IS THE SAME. THE COURT MUST FINALIZE THE RIGHTS AND RESPONSIBILITIES OF THE MOTHER AND FATHER BASED UPON WHAT IS IN THE BEST INTEREST OF THE BABY.

IF HE DENIED THE BABY AT FIRST, CAN HE GET VISITATION RIGHTS?

THE COURT MUST DECIDE WHO WILL HAVE CUSTODY OF THE BABY AND WHAT VISITATION RIGHTS THERE WILL BE. A PARENT WILL BE DENIED VISITATION ONLY IF IT WOULD BE HARMFUL TO THE CHILD IN SOME WAY. IT IS ALMOST ALWAYS BETTER FOR THE BABY TO HAVE A LOVING RELATIONSHIP WITH BOTH PARENTS. THE FACT THAT THE FATHER DIDN'T ADMIT THE BABY WAS HIS WILL NOT BE HELD AGAINST HIM.

I WANT THE BABY TO HAVE MY NAME.

THE COURT WILL USUALLY GO ALONG WITH ANY NAME THE MOTHER AND FATHER AGREE TO. IF THERE IS NO AGREEMENT, THE COURT DECIDES, AFTER HEARING TESTIMONY, WHAT WILL BE BEST FOR THE BABY.

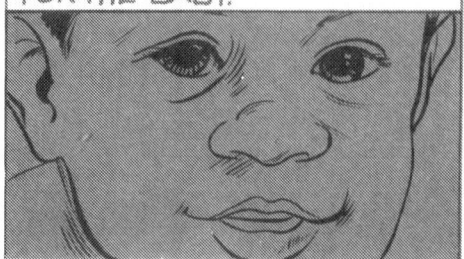

MY BABY HAS A LOT OF MEDICAL BILLS. WHO HAS TO PAY FOR THEM?

AFTER HEARING EVIDENCE, THE COURT WILL DECIDE WHO SHOULD PAY. IT CAN ORDER THE FATHER OR MOTHER TO BE RESPONSIBLE FOR BIRTH EXPENSES, OTHER MEDICAL OR DENTAL COSTS, AND INSURANCE.

WHAT ABOUT CHILD SUPPORT FOR MY CHILD.

USUALLY THE PARENT NOT HAVING CUSTODY OF THE CHILD IS ORDERED TO PAY CHILD SUPPORT. THE SUPPORT PAYMENTS ARE PAID TO THE CLERK'S OFFICE SO THAT THERE WILL BE A PERMANENT RECORD OF ALL PAYMENTS. THE COURT WILL DECIDE HOW MUCH THE SUPPORT WILL BE.

I GO TO SCHOOL FULL-TIME AND DON'T HAVE A JOB. WILL I STILL HAVE TO PAY CHILD SUPPORT?

THE COURT MUST DO WHAT IS BEST FOR THE BABY. YOU WILL BE ORDERED TO PAY SOME CHILD SUPPORT.

HOW MUCH DO I HAVE TO PAY?

THE COURT MUST DETERMINE FIRST WHAT THE NEEDS OF THE CHILD ARE, AND WHAT SOURCES OF INCOME ARE AVAILABLE TO YOU AND THE MOTHER. IT WILL ATTEMPT TO SET A FAIR AMOUNT OF SUPPORT. THE COURT RECOGNIZES, THOUGH, HOW IMPORTANT AN EDUCATION IS, AND WILL TRY TO WORK WITH YOU SO THAT YOU CAN PAY SUPPORT AND STAY IN SCHOOL.

WHAT IF HE GETS BEHIND IN SUPPORT PAYMENTS, OR JUST REFUSES TO PAY?
THERE ARE SEVERAL WAYS TO FORCE HIM TO PAY SUPPORT. HIS SUPPORT CAN BE ORDERED WITHHELD FROM HIS PAYCHECK, HIS TAX REFUND CHECK COULD BE TAKEN, OR FINALLY HE COULD BE SENT TO JAIL.
IF I DON'T HAVE A REGULAR JOB, HOW CAN I PAY SUPPORT? I WON'T BE ABLE TO GET A JOB OR PAY SUPPORT IF I'M IN JAIL.
PUTTING SOMEONE IN JAIL FOR CONTEMPT OF COURT IS A LAST RESORT. AS LONG AS YOU CONVINCE THE COURT YOU'RE MAKING AN HONEST EFFORT BY PAYING SOMETHING EVERY WEEK AND SHOWING PROOF OF LOOKING FOR A JOB FOR EXAMPLE, YOU PROBABLY WILL NOT GO TO JAIL.
THIS ALL SOUNDS SCARY AND VERY COMPLICATED, IS IT REALLY WORTH ALL THE TROUBLE?
ONLY YOU CAN DECIDE THAT, BUT YOU MUST THINK OF WHAT'S BEST FOR YOUR BABY, NOT WHAT'S BEST FOR YOU. THE BABY'S RIGHTS OF SUPPORT, MEDICAL ASSISTANCE AND INHERITANCE CAN ONLY BE ENFORCED IF PATERNITY IS ESTABLISHED.
CAN I WAIT A FEW YEARS TO DO THIS?
PROBABLY, BUT YOU SHOULD KNOW THAT YOU MAY LOSE SOME OF YOUR RIGHTS IF YOU WAIT TOO LONG. IN ALMOST EVERY CASE, WAITING ONLY MAKES IT MORE DIFFICULT TO HAVE PATERNITY ESTABLISHED.

CAN I HAVE PATERNITY ESTABLISHED IF THE BABY'S MOTHER WON'T COOPERATE?
INDIANA LAW PROVIDES THAT YOU ALSO HAVE A RIGHT TO PROVE YOU ARE THE FATHER.
WHAT IF I'M ONLY SIXTEEN YEARS OLD?
IF EITHER YOU OR THE FATHER IS NOT YET EIGHTEEN YEARS OF AGE, YOU MUST HAVE A PARENT OR GUARDIAN OR RELATIVE, AT LEAST 18 YEARS OF AGE, TO ASSIST IN ESTABLISHING PATERNITY.
CAN'T WE JUST SIGN A PAPER OR SOMETHING TO HAVE PATERNITY ESTABLISHED?
NO. YOU MUST HAVE PATERNITY ESTABLISHED BY A COURT OF LAW.
DO YOU REALLY THINK ESTABLISHING PATERNITY IS IMPORTANT?
IT'S OF GREAT IMPORTANCE TO YOUR CHILD. YOU OWE IT TO YOUR CHILD AND TO YOURSELF TO GET AS MUCH INFORMATION ABOUT PATERNITY AS POSSIBLE, AND CAREFULLY CONSIDER WHAT WILL BE BEST FOR YOUR BABY, BOTH TODAY AND IN THE COMING YEARS.

SUMMARY

All parents, regardless of their age, are responsible for the support of their children. When a child is born to unmarried parents, paternity—legally naming the father of the child—can be established in many ways. The alleged father may voluntarily admit paternity. The child, mother, father, child support offices, or welfare (AFDC) may begin legal proceedings.

It is important for teen parents to weigh the pros and cons of paternity establishment. It is very important to understand the benefits of paternity for the child. Many diseases and other medical conditions are passed to children by their parents.

Paternity interviews with the mother and alleged father(s) can be emotionally draining. You may wish to have someone accompany you. Also, if you are named the father in a paternity matter, you need to know how to protect and enforce your legal rights.

Issues for Teen Parents:

- Why would a young unwed mother not pursue paternity? What are reasons a young unwed father would not admit paternity? What are the pros and cons?
- Know the benefits of paternity for the child, parents, grandparents, and society.

Chapter IV

This chapter explains how to get support in the family courts for yourself and your children. While it will provide you with helpful information, it is not a substitute for a lawyer. It gives you only general information, not legal advice about your personal situation. It is almost always better to have a lawyer when you go to court for support. Many teen parents cannot afford a lawyer. Legal assistance may be available to you at no cost. Whether or not you have a lawyer, it is important that you know as much as possible about the system.

This chapter will:

- Describe the services your child support office provides.
- Discuss how the family court (domestic relations court) can help teen parents.
- Identify the roles of officials involved in child support enforcement.

Support in the Family Courts

This child support program is intended to help parents to meet their responsibility to support their children—even if the father has never lived with them. **Both parents have an obligation to support their children—regardless of the age of the parents.** The child support program must provide free services to all welfare-recipient families when the non-custodial parent is alive but absent from the home.

You do not have to go on public assistance to receive child support services. All states are required to provide the same services to nonwelfare that they provide to welfare families. Nonwelfare families must make an application for services, and there may be a small fee (up to $25) charged at the time of application.

Your child support office will represent the interests of the minor children of teen parents in child support actions. Services available from the child support office include:

- Determining who the parents are.
- Locating a child's parents for the purpose of establishing paternity and/or child support.
- Establishing and enforcing a court order to pay child support.
- Collecting child support payments.
- Establishing or continuing medical support.

UNDERSTANDING ROLES IN CHILD SUPPORT ENFORCEMENT

JUDGE:

The judge will listen to your story. He listens to the parties and evaluates the needs of the children. He makes the decisions: whom the child will live with, who is the father of the child, what are the visitation rights, and how much child support should be paid. In paternity matters, the judge may order blood testing.

MASTER, REFEREE, or HEARING OFFICER:

In some courts the orders are not made by a judge, but by a "master," a "referee," or a "hearing officer." Their role is similar to a judge's, but they do not have all his authority. Their orders must be approved and signed by the judge.

PROSECUTOR or DISTRICT ATTORNEY:

The prosecutor or district attorney will follow the case until the child support moneys are collected. If paternity is not voluntarily admitted by the alleged father, it may be pursued by the prosecutor. He may also represent the child support office in enforcing child support.

GUARDIAN:

If the mother or father (alleged father) of the child for whom support is sought is not of the age of majority (in most states the age is 18), she or he must have someone of legal age to help protect her or his rights. Often the judge may appoint a parent as the minor's legal guardian. The parent is responsible for making decisions and controlling your legal interests. States vary in the legal protections offered to minor fathers in defending against claims of paternity.

COURT PERSONNEL:

On the day of a court hearing, the bailiff will call the case. It is his job to make sure all the parties are ready when the judge is ready. He may also administer the oath to the parties. If someone becomes too emotional or loud in the courtroom, the bailiff may call for "order in the court!" or request assistance from a sheriff's officer. The court reporter is also in the courtroom. Everything said in court is "on the record."

PROBATION OFFICER:

In may counties the probation officer has the responsibility for enforcing child support orders. This unit may be called a "support collection unit."

WELFARE PERSONNEL:

When a custodial parent (she or he who has custody of the child) is unable to provide for the child, he or she may apply for welfare. All applicants for welfare are screened to make sure they qualify for assistance. The welfare office may begin court action for support of the child.

When you go to the child support office, you may be asked to provide as much of the following information as possible:

- Full legal name and address of the parent who is obligated to pay support.

- Date of birth and physical description or photographs of the other parent.

- Other parent's social security number. Child(ren)'s birth certificates.

- Marriage license or divorce or separation agreement if you have one.
- Name and address of the current or most recent employer of the father.
- Names of friends and relatives of the noncustodial parent and any organizations to which he or she may belong.
- Any information you may have regarding the noncustodial parent's income or assets: pay slips, tax returns, cars, boats, investments, or property.

The more complete, reliable, and accurate the information, the easier it is to collect child support for your child.

What Is the Family Court?

The family court, or domestic relations court, is county-based, so the parent should go to the court in the county in which either or both live. The family court handles many family problems. It has the power to make orders of support and to establish paternity. The family court can also issue restraining orders for people who are in danger from other members of the family. The court can decide matters of child abuse, termination of parental rights, child custody, visitation, guardianship, and adoption.

In the family court you generally may represent yourself without a lawyer. The court should provide staff to explain the procedures and help you fill out the necessary forms.

Your case may be heard by the court's hearing examiner. The examiner handles only support matters, and his decisions can be reviewed by a judge.

How Much Support?

In deciding how much support a parent must pay, the court will often use the state child support guidelines. They are based on the income and property of the parent. Both parents must support their children, even if the parents were never married.

In order to collect child support from the father, you will have to prove in court that he is indeed the father. Even if he admits to fathering the child, you may still have to go to court to seek an order that legally establishes paternity. You may request child support at the same time. To bring a paternity action, you must file a petition (a sworn statement). In order to receive public assistance, you are required to cooperate with the welfare office in paternity establishment unless you have a good cause not to do so.

If the alleged father denies that the child is his, the mother may file a petition, and the courts will try to determine the legal father. The court may order blood tests. Proving paternity can sometimes be tricky. You will need medical records to show when you became pregnant and witnesses or papers (letters from the alleged father, for example) proving your relationship.

Many courts will not pursue paternity and child support if the alleged father is under 18 years of age, a full-time student, and unemployed. They prefer to wait until he is 18 years old and fully employed. Other courts, however, will order a "token payment" of $5 or $10 a week to help the young father understand his repsonsibilities for his child.

Child Support and Public Assistance

You can get child support for yourself and your child even if you are receiving public assistance. If you are getting more public assistance than the father is paying in child support, most of his payments will go to the department of social services as reimbursement. But you should receive the first $50 of the father's payment each month. Once you are no longer receiving welfare, all child support moneys will be sent to you by the child support unit.

Preparing Your Case

Before you go to family court, you should gather as much information as possible. It is important to have the address and social security number of the other parent so that he or she can be ordered to appear in court. Your goal is to convince the court that you need support and that the other parent can provide it. The more evidence you have of your needs and the other parent's ability to pay, the better chance you have of receiving a favorable decision.

CHILD SUPPORT INFORMATION CHECKLIST

Personal information about the other parent:

- Home and work address
- Social security number
- Kind of work
- Education
- Union or trade association membership
- Driver's license
- Date of birth

Expenses: Yours and the Child's

- Rent, mortgage, maintenance
- Utilities (gas, electric, telephone)
- Food (include lunches at work or school)
- Clothing
- Entertainment
- Cleaning, laundry
- Travel expenses to work, school, day care, doctors
- Child care
- Medical, drugs, and dental expenses
- Special expenses

Documents: For Both Parents

- Child's birth certificate
- Three most recent pay stubs
- All monthly bills including overdue bills or anything else to prove your income or lack of income

Going to Court

Allow yourself plenty of time so that you can arrive at court early. Try to leave your child with a friend or at the day care center. He or she may become bored and restless if you bring them. Make sure you have all the necessary documents. Both parents should bring in proof of their expenses (if any) and pay receipts if they are working.

Show your respect and maturity by dressing well. Don't wear a T-shirt and ragged jeans. You are trying to make a good impression. You should be brief and not talk about anything other than your support needs and the other parent's ability to pay support. You may wish to discuss what you plan to say in advance with a friend.

The court officer at the entrance to the court will direct you to the right waiting room. When you get there look for the calendar. It will usually be on a wall near the courtroom door. It is a list of the names of people whose cases will be heard in that courtroom. If your name is not on the calendar, you should tell the court officer and show him or her your copy of your court notice.

Once you are sure that you are in the right place, relax. You may have to wait for several hours. Listen for your name or the other parent's name. **Do not leave the waiting room, even for a minute, without telling the court officer.** If you miss your name because you went to the rest room, your case could be dismissed. **Don't leave!**

When your case is called, you will be shown into the courtroom. It is normal to feel scared. Remember, every person in that courtroom is just another person like you. The court staff are there to help you. The courts, however, are often very crowded, and the judge or hearing officer may be in a hurry to finish. But despite backlogs, they are responsible for listening to both sides of the case and giving both sides time to explain their needs.

When you enter the courtroom the clerk will tell you where to stand. The procedure in family court is informal, but you should always show respect. The hearing examiner or judge may greet you by saying, for example, "Good morning." You should respond in kind with, "Good morning, your honor." You will be asked to raise your right hand and swear to the truth of what you are about to say. The court reporter will ask for your address. Speak up so that you can be heard.

If you have information that shows your income and expenses, you may give it to the court officer, Say, "Your honor, I would like you to look at this list of the other parent's income and my expenses." If you know how much money the father is earning, tell this to the court. If the father refuses to pay his child support, you may ask to have it deducted from his pay.

Remember, you should always be polite in court. Say what is important, and don't whisper or mumble. The judge has the final word. Never interrupt the judge. If he refuses to listen, leave the courtroom quietly.

If you feel that the hearing examiner's decision was unfair, you may file an objection. It will be reviewed by a judge who will decide if the hearing examiner was correct.

After the hearing is over, you will be told where to go to get a copy of your child support order. You should read it carefully to make sure everything is correct. Since many parents often disobey their support orders, you should keep records of support payments as they are made. Usually the child support unit will keep records for you, but they may make mistakes.

If in the future your situation changes or the other parent's situation changes so that they can pay more, you may request a change in your support order. Also, a parent paying child support may request a decrease if a change in his circumstances justifies it.

> A summons is a notice for you to appear in court and should not be ignored. If it is, the judge may set a new date for the court hearing and issue a warrant for your arrest.

Order of Protection

A Restraining Order, or Order of Protection, may be necessary to protect you and your child. For example, suppose the father of the child threatens or harasses you. You may ask for a hearing at which the judge will try to determine what is going on. In court, speaking audibly, calmly, and clearly, tell what the other party did to you, and describe your injuries and fears. Answer the judge's questions briefly. Do not show anger with what the judge asks or says. If you're upset, don't be ashamed to cry.

Never argue with or interrupt the judge! Talk only with the judge. Do not talk to, argue with, or interrupt the other party, no matter what the other party says.

The judge may order the other party to stay away from you and the child. If the other party violates the restraining order, you may call the police and have him arrested. An individual arrested for violating a restraining order will have a right to a lawyer.

Custody and Visitation

Legal custody of a child means that the courts have said that you have the right to decide how to raise your child. You also have the right to have your child with you if you have legal custody. Both the mother and the father have an equal right to custody unless the court orders otherwise. If, however, the parents were not married when the child was born, the father does not have equal rights to custody until the court establishes paternity.

Importance of Legal Custody

Just because your child lives with you does not mean you have legal custody, only physical custody. Either parent can ask the court to grant legal custody. You have the edge if legal custody is requested while the child is living with you. If you do not have a legal custody order, the other parent may have the right to take the child away from you.

The judge must decide what is in the child's best interests. The judge will look at your living conditions and the abilities of each parent to make decisions. The judge will also look at the emotional ties between the parents and the child. Just because one parent has more money than the other does not mean that that parent will get custody. The judge may also order the parents to take psychological tests. Custody may be changed at a later date if the other parent shows that the situation has changed and the child would be better off with that parent.

How Do I Get Visitation?

If the other parent has custody, you have the right to visitation. This will be defined in your court order. The court may set specific dates, times, and places for you to visit your child. You may have weekday and/or weekend visits. You may also be able to have the child with you in your home.

If the parents were not married when the child was born, the father must have the courts determine that he, in fact, is the legal father. Then a visitation order will be made.

Grandparents may have visitation rights with their grandchildren. In Michigan and Wisconsin, grandparents also have certain legal and financial responsibilities for the grandchildren born of minor parents.

Understanding Your Court Order

A court order shows how much is to be paid and when. It includes the terms of custody, visitation, and other parental rights. If both parents voluntarily agree to a court order, they may sign a consent agreement which the court will approve. If you cannot reach an agreement, the case will be scheduled for court and a judge will decide. If the noncustodial parent is able to provide medical coverage at little or no cost, it will be included in the court order. It is important to understand that a court order in one state is enforceable throughout the 50 states.

Enforcing Your Court Order

One of the main purposes of the child support program is to make sure that the obligated parent obeys his court order and makes his child support payments regularly and in the correct amount. When a parent doesn't pay the entire amount or doesn't pay at all, enforcement action is necessary.

The child support office may have the payment deducted from the obligated parent's wages. If he is in the military, payments can be taken directly out of his paycheck. If he is behind in his child support, his state and federal income tax refunds can be taken by the child support office. Even if he is collecting unemployment benefits, a certain amount can be taken out of his pay for child support.

Grandparent's Responsibility

In all 50 states, both parents are responsible for the support of their children. In most states, other relatives are not responsible under the law for helping to support children. Michigan and Wisconsin, however, have laws that make grandparents financially responsible for supporting infants born to their minor children. Many feel these laws are not working. Many feel they are unfair.

One criticism is that support of a grandchild begins when paternity is established. This may take so long that the teen father has turned 18 by the time paternity is established. Also, almost half of the fathers of teen mothers are not minors, a fact that may affect the mother's eligibility for public assistance. Those who support grandparent liability believe that it will force teens to behave more reponsibly out of fear that their parents will have to pay support.

Looking beyond teenage pregnancy

Some facts about the financial responsibilities of parenthood

"For a teenager, having a child is an expensive problem that lasts a lifetime."

"Children need love and support **from both parents.**"

This flier, prepared by the Georgia Department of Human Resources, will help you understand your rights and responsibilities for the support of your children.

Suppose I don't make a lot of money. **How much** will the Child Support Office take?

If you are already under a court order, the office of Child Support Enforcement will collect the amount due under the order (up to **50%** of your wages can be garnisheed). If not, they will give you some say if you talk with them and make voluntary arrangements. They will consider your ability to pay in determining the amount you should pay each month. You will have to pay back the welfare payments and keep your child support payments up to date. That can take many years.

I've heard my child's father **won't have to pay** child support. He's in the **Army.**

That is **not true.** When you give information about him to the child support agent, the agent will contact the military authorities and make arrangements for child support payments.

But **suppose I have a lot of bills,** car payments and payments on my stereo?

Child support must come first. Children are their parents' responsibility. You might have to give up the car or the stereo—or both.

I don't want to go through all this. **My parents** will take care of the baby and I'm going back to school. Why should I try to get child support?

As your child grows up, he or she has a right to be loved and supported by **both** parents. Unless certain legal steps are taken, your child **will not have a legal father** and **will not get** the support and **rights of inheritance** from both parents.

Can't I get welfare (Aid to Families with Dependent Children) to help me take care of my baby? I don't want to get married.

You may, but you must help your caseworker identify the father and get him to help pay the child's expenses.

How will the State find out who the father is?

The mother must give all the personal information she has about the father to the caseworker before she can draw welfare for herself and her child. **Blood tests** are used by office of Child Support Enforcement to determine who may or may not be the father of the child. Tests include blood samples from the possible father, the mother and the baby; and they are very accurate. A person who does not believe he is the father can also ask for blood tests. The Office of Child Support Enforcement has agents who will talk with the father and mother and help arrange the payments.

I **can't** pay child support. I'm in school and **I don't have a job.**

The State Child Support program, under the Kentucky Cabinet for Human Resources, may help your child and the mother. But you are building up a **debt** with every welfare payment they get—and **you will have to pay it back. That's the law.** Parents have the primary responsibility. Welfare is a substitute.

I'm the baby's father, but I'm in school. I only have an afternoon job for spending money. Who knows where I'll be by the time I make enough to pay child support. **How can the state find me when even I don't know where I'll be living?**

The Child Support Office will find you. Every state has an office to locate absent parents. The federal government has a **nationwide network** to locate absent parents. They use public records such as social security numbers, labor records, unemployment records, driver's license records and car registration records to find parents who should be paying support and paying back the welfare money "borrowed" in welfare payments.

SUMMARY

The child support program helps parents in many ways. This includes locating parents in order to establish paternity/child support and establishing and enforcing child support orders. These services are provided free to all welfare-recipient families when the noncustodial parent is alive but absent from the home. Nonwelfare families must make an application for services, and there may be a small fee.

The family/domestic relations courts deal with many of the legal problems your family may have. They can decide matters of child abuse, custody, visitation, child support, guardianship, and adoption. It is important to prepare for court and dress properly. Never argue or interrupt the judge. You may address him as "your honor."

Issues for Teen Parents:

- What are ways the family court can help teen parents? Where is the family court located in your community?
- What are steps that teen parents can take in preparing for court?
- What is the importance of legal custody, visitation rights, and an order of protection for teen parents?
- How do you feel about grandparents being legally responsible for the support of their grandchildren when the parents are minors?

Chapter V

Welfare is not charity. It is a government program designed to help people who don't have other ways to support themselves or their families. It provides money to families with children until they can earn enough money to support themselves. Many people refer to this as their "county check" or "welfare check." It provides money every month to eligible children for food, clothing, shelter, and living expenses.

This chapter will:

- Describe several problems teen parents have in applying for social services.
- Prepare you for an interview with the welfare (AFDC) department.
- Explain why teen parents may be denied benefits for which they are eligible.

Teen Parents and Welfare

> **CAUTION: WELFARE RULES CHANGE**
> Welfare rules change all the time. Many of the rules discussed in this book may have changed by the time you read it. If something seems to have changed or you have any questions, check with a social worker or a knowledgeable friend or counselor.

The term *welfare* involves three programs: Aid to Families with Dependent Children (AFDC), medicaid, and food stamps. AFDC provides cash assistance. Medicaid provides health care services. Food stamps are coupons that can be used only for the purchase of food.

The welfare program is a large source of public support for teenage mothers and their children. The program provides cash assistance to needy women who are eligible by being the female head of a household with children under 18. If you are an unmarried teenager who is unemployed or has a very limited income, your child is likely to qualify for welfare, food stamps, and medicaid. The mother may or may not be eligible, depending on the income and resources of her own parents since they are responsible for her while she is 18 or under.

A woman pregnant with her first child is not eligible for cash payments until the last four months of her pregnancy. Some states may extend medicaid coverage prior to the time when the welfare benefit can be paid so that prenatal care may be obtained.

Problems Teen Parents Have in Applying for Social Services

- Many young parents do not understand their legal rights. They rely too heavily on friends and "street talk" for information about the "system."
- Young parents may be confused by the various rules, procedures, guidelines, and paperwork.
- They may have difficulty obtaining the required documents.
- They may not have the patience for long waits and delays.
- They may not have adequate transportation for getting to and from the welfare office.
- They may have language difficulties or handicaps that present certain problems.
- Caseworkers at the welfare office may not take the time to communicate effectively and sensitively about their rights.
- Many young parents find it difficult to respond to personal questions regarding their sexual behavior.
- Teen mothers are concerned about the cash grant being sent directly to the child's grandmother and not distributed fairly to the mother and her child. They also worry that if the grandmother's income is too high, they won't get a cash grant for the baby.

> It is important to remember that many teen mothers are trying to raise their children under difficult economic and social circumstances. Not all teen mothers are unemployed or go on welfare. Not all teen mothers who go on welfare will stay there indefinitely.

Policies for Welfare Services

"Assistance is to be administered promptly and humanely, with due regard to the preservation of family life without discrimination on account of race, color, national origin, religion, political affiliation, sex, or marital status. Assistance is to be administered so as to encourage self-respect, self-reliance, and the desire to be a good citizen who is useful to society.

"It is the responsibility of all who are concerned with the administration of aid to do so with courtesy, consideration, and respect toward applicants and recipients and without attempting to elicit unnecessary information. **Duties should be performed in such a way as to secure for every applicant and recipient the amount of aid to which he or she is entitled under the law.**

"All applications and records are confidential and not open to examination for any purpose not directly connected with the administration of these programs.

"Applications for public assistance are to be reviewed promptly in accordance with regulations.

"The county is responsible for assisting applicants or recipients in understanding their rights and responsibilities and for assisting them as needed in establishing their eligibility and helping them to realize the maximum personal independence of which they are capable, including self-care and self-maintenance."

Application Process for Welfare

The exact procedures may vary depending on the state in which you live. In order to get welfare and food stamps you must apply at your local welfare office. On your first visit you may be given an "applications packet" and told what papers to bring for your next appointment. The interviewer should give you an appointment to come back not more than five workdays later. You have the right to complete the application even if the interviewer thinks you are not eligible. It is important that you read everything in the application carefully. If you are unable to answer certain questions, ask the welfare worker to help you. They are responsible for helping you to complete the application. **Also, if you have an emergency situation, tell them right away!**

When a teen mother is already on her mother's welfare grant, she may have very limited contact with the welfare agency. Where young parents do have contact with a social service agency, they may wish to have a responsible friend or relative accompany them to the interview. The welfare worker will explain the agency requirements and program limitations as well as the applicant's rights and responsibilities. If you indicate that you have an emergency situation, the agency will make a determination of whether an immediate problem exists.

Whether a teenage mother is eligible for welfare will depend on whether she lives on her own or with her parents, whether her mother is receiving welfare, whether she is under 18 or over 18 years of age, and whether she is pregnant or has given birth at the time of application.

The vast majority of teenage mothers who are pregnant or have children live with their parents. According to the Department of Health and Human Services, only 3% of the welfare households are headed by teenagers 18 and under. Under current regulations, when a teen parent under age 18 applies for public assistance for herself and her child, and the teen's parents reside in the same household, the grandparents' income is to be deemed available for the needs of both the teen parent and her child.

Often young parents are reluctant to seek assistance until the problem becomes a crisis. Young parents may have an emergency need for food and shelter. They may need crisis intervention and legal assistance, counseling, education, and job training. They may need medical care for themselves and their children.

Family Welfare Reform Act

This represents the most significant change in the welfare system since it began in 1935. The bill strengthens child support enforcement and extends child care and Medicaid services to families for one year after a parent has left AFDC for work outside the home.

Some advocates for pregnant and parenting teens believe that many teen parents will not benefit from these changes. They contend that for teen parents living at home, their parent's income is deemed available to them whether or not it is used for support. The result is often a reduced grant or no grant at all. A basic understanding of the AFDC rules will help you to obtain the benefits to which you are entitled.

> Young parents need advice on how to protect their rights and receive the benefits to which they are entitled. They need to know what to do when they are not treated fairly. For many teenage mothers and their children, welfare and other social services such as food stamps, WIC, and medicaid are an important bridge that allows them to cope and regroup before moving toward independence.

The AFDC Check:

- Will be sent once each month.
- Will be made payable to the eligible relative taking care of the dependent children.
- May be cashed only by an eligible relative after presenting proper identification.
- May not be issued unless the eligible relative has signed a statement that he or she has given the department true and complete information.

Grant Amount

Each state sets a grant level based on an estimate of the minimum amount necessary to meet a family's basic needs. The grant level changes with family size.

> "Eligibility for welfare is determined in terms of family income. A pregnant or parenting teen must know whether she and her baby will be considered a self-contained family or whether the income of other relatives will be taken into account."

Your First Welfare Interview

You should take to your first interview:

- Your birth certificate, baptismal record, or evidence of birth.
- Pregnancy verification: county form or statement signed by doctor.
- Social security number for yourself and any children. (If you don't have one, you must agree to get one.)
- All known information about father(s) of child(ren) born or unborn.
- If you are a minor and not residing with your parents, the names and addresses of your parents.
- Proof of value for any items of real or personal property—e.g., checking or savings accounts.
- Vehicle registration card and proof of amount owed.
- Alien registration card, if appropriate.
- Proof of any income being received—e.g., wage stubs, if employed; award letters for any benefits such as social security (deceased or disabled parent) or Supplemental Security Income (SSI) (personal disability).

If food stamps are being applied for, also take:

- Rent receipt or similar proof of amount paid for housing.
- Knowledge of which utilities you are required to pay.
- Name of person and amount of income received by any person(s) who lives with you.

THINGS TO KNOW:

- Your street address and telephone number.
- If you are receiving AFDC or any other public assistance such as medicaid, food stamps, or SSI.
- If you have any medical insurance coverage for yourself and/or your child.
- If your parent or relative caretaker is receiving AFDC or any other assistance.

Application Steps

- Apply at the county welfare office. You may wish to go with a friend or relative.

- Ask the receptionist for an application. Fill out as many questions as you can. If you are unable to answer certain questions, you may ask for help in filling out the forms.

- Turn in the application and wait for an appointment to see an eligibility worker.

- Have the necessary documents already mentioned with you.

- Except for emergency situations (immediate-need checks), you will not receive your benefits until all information is in your eligibility folder. If you have trouble getting the necessary documents, ask for help from your eligibility worker.

- If you are told you don't qualify, you still have a right to submit a written application.

- You should write down your eligibility worker's name and phone number and what times to telephone. Personally bring in all the additional requested papers. If you have to mail the papers, it is a good idea to ask your worker for a stamped envelope addressed to him or her.

- **Always take change (quarters, dimes, nickels) with you in case you need to make a telephone call while you are at the social service agency. You may need to call a counselor if there is a problem and your application is not processed.**

- Keep a record for yourself and keep all your papers.

- Monthly reports: Each month you must fill out a monthly report that comes in the mail with your first check of the month. The purpose of this form is to report whether your situation is the same or has changed. The form needs to be mailed back promptly. If it is not returned by the date indicated, your AFDC benefits will not continue after a certain date.

What Is Meant by "Cooperation"?

The law requires you to cooperate with welfare and child support agencies unless you have good cause for noncooperation. The welfare caseworker will ask the mother questions about the alleged father's identity and location. This interview may be stressful and difficult for you, so you may wish to take a friend or relative along. In cooperation with the welfare or child support agency, you may be asked to do one or more of the following:

- Name the absent parent of any child applying for or receiving AFDC, and give information you have to help find the parent.
- Help to determine legally who the father is if your child was born out of wedlock.
- Pay to the Department of Social Services any money that is given directly to you by the absent parent.

You may be required to go to the welfare office, child support office, or court to sign papers or give the necessary information. You will be asked to sign a statement under penalty of perjury on any information or lack of information you have about the alleged father.

What Is Meant by "Good Cause"?

You may have a good cause not to cooperate in identifying the father. You may be excused from cooperating if you believe that cooperation is not in the best interest of your child and provide evidence to support this claim.

If You Do Not Cooperate and You Do Not Have a Good Cause:

- You will be ineligible for welfare.
- Your children will still be eligible for AFDC for their own needs.
- Your children's grants will go to another person, called a "protective payee."

How and When to Claim Good Cause

If you want to claim good cause, you must tell a worker that you think you have good cause. You can do this at any time that you believe you have good cause not to cooperate. The following are the circumstances under which the welfare agency may determine that you have good cause for refusing to cooperate:

- **Cooperation is anticipated to result in serious physical or emotional harm to the child.**

- **Cooperation is anticipated to result in physical or emotional harm to you which is so serious that it reduces your ability to care for the child adequately.**

- **The child was born after forcible rape or incest.**

- **Court proceedings are going on for adoption of the child.**

- **You are working with an agency that is helping you to decide whether to place the child for adoption.**

It is the parent's responsibility to provide the welfare agency with the evidence needed to determine whether there is good cause for refusing to cooperate. The welfare agency may decide your claim on the basis of evidence you give them. They may conduct an investigation to verify your claim further.

> **CAUTION**
>
> Teen parents should be careful. You may be denied benefits for which you are eligible. There are many reasons why this happens:
>
> - Arithmetic errors.
> - Communication problems between the applicant and eligibility worker.
> - Confusion in regulations or misinterpretation.
> - Missing information that is available.
> - The system is overloaded due to cutbacks.

None of these is a good reason for denying your rights under the law. Many problems and disputes can come up at your interview. The welfare worker may refuse to give you emergency food stamps or issue a temporary check. They may insist on information you have no way of getting. Your welfare worker can make mistakes.

Right to Appeal

If you feel your case was improperly handled, you have a right to appeal whereby a service representative will investigate the situation. You are also entitled to a FAIR HEARING before a hearing officer. The hearing officer will decide if you were wronged in the way the welfare agency handled your case. The hearing officer will listen to you and the person from the welfare agency explain the situation. He then decides the dispute. Remember that the whole process was created to protect the rights of those who are eligible for these programs.

TIPS FOR DEALING WITH SOCIAL SERVICE AGENCIES

- Read all letters and forms carefully. If something doesn't make sense, get help in understanding it.

- Keep notes of when and with whom you speak.

- Keep your cool! The welfare workers are often under a lot of pressure. They deal with a lot of complicated rules and paperwork. It's not an easy job. Try not to get angry over problems and delays.

- Keep appointments. Your case can be closed immediately if you miss or are late for an appointment.

- Immediately request a fair hearing if you feel your rights have been violated.

- Be persistent. In a welfare office there is a chain of command. If you feel you worker is doing something wrong, ask to speak with the supervisor. Contact a community agency or legal aid for help.

- Save all records, letters, notes, and documents.

Young Fathers and Welfare

A young unwed father may also qualify for welfare and other services. He may be eligible if he is a dependent child living with his parents or a caretaker relative and is under 18 years of age (or at state option, 19 if he is in school). He may receive benefits if he is living with his child and the child's mother, if he or the child's mother is incapacitated, or if he qualifies for the Unemployed Parent Program that is available in some states. A young unwed father with custody of his child may also file for basic AFDC benefits on behalf of himself and his child.

Work Requirements and Welfare

Work requirements for welfare vary and are in a state of change. Generally, young mothers do not have to register for work if they are caring for a young child. If you are a full-time student, you may not have to register for work. Many young mothers and fathers are eager to participate in job programs that make them more employable.

Generally, you don't have to take a job for the following reasons:

- Employer doesn't have a license.
- Employer doesn't pay unemployment compensation or unemployment insurance.
- Employer violates health and safety regulations.
- Employer pays less than the customary wage for that work set by the state or the minimun wage, whichever is higher.

- You are ill.
- No child-care arrangements can be made.
- Taking the job would prevent you from completing an approved training program.

College Students and Welfare

If you are going to college while you are receiving AFDC you may be eligible for special grants to pay for tuition, books, supplies, child care, and other essential items if you are unable to pay for them any other way. To apply for these grants, you must provide the welfare office with documents that establish your eligibility.

You will have to show where you are going to school, how long the course will last, what dates you will attend, exactly what courses you are taking, and what kinds of jobs you will qualify for when you graduate. You will have to show the costs of all items that you need a special grant to pay. And you will have to demonstrate that you do not have enough student financial aid to cover your tuition, books, supplies, and other items requested in your grant.

SUMMARY

Welfare (Aid to Families with Dependent Children) is not charity. It is a government program that provides money to families with children until they can earn enough money to support themselves. Applying for welfare and protecting your rights while receiving AFDC can involve a great deal of time and effort.

The term **welfare** involves three programs: AFDC, medicaid, and food stamps. The welfare program is a large source of public support for teenage mothers and their children.

Teen parents often have problems in applying for social services. It is important that you know how to protect and enforce your rights. This is especially true for young mothers who are required to cooperate in naming the father of their child.

Generally speaking, when you receive welfare, you assign your rights to child support to the state.

Issues for Teen Parents:

- What problems and concerns do teen parents have when applying for welfare? What documents should you bring with you for a welfare interview?

- What rights does a teen mother have for claiming a "good cause" in not identifying the father of her child when applying for welfare (AFDC)?

- Describe how teen parents can be denied benefits to which they are entitled. What steps can you take to avoid these problems?

Chapter VI

Food stamps are government coupons provided to increase the food purchasing power of low-income households to the point where they can purchase a low-cost diet that is nutritionally adequate. Food stamps are available to all households if they meet eligibility requirements. Even married couples are eligible.

This chapter will:

- Help you to understand how food stamps and Women, Infants, and Children (WIC) can help teenagers.
- Describe how to apply for food stamps and WIC.

Food Stamps

If you qualify you can pay for some of your food with the assistance of government coupons called "food stamps." Most teen parents will have to spend cash as well as their food stamps in order to have enough food. Almost all food stores will take food stamps. Food stamps can be used to buy any foods; however, they cannot be used for most restaurant foods, tobacco products, alcohol, and pet foods.

You apply for food stamps by filling out an application form at your county welfare office. Go to your welfare office, and they will give you an application right away. They will review your application and have 30 days to act on your application and provide you with food stamps if you are eligible. **If your income is very low and you have an urgent need, you may be eligible for emergency food stamps which may be received in most cases within 5 days.**

Households receiving AFDC are automatically eligible for food stamps. All other applicants must meet certain limits on money and property. Generally, teen parents who are under 16 or are caring for a child under 6 years of age do not have to register for work and are eligible for food stamps.

If you need immediate help you may be eligible for "expedited service" by meeting any of the following conditions:

- All members of the household are homeless.
- Your monthly costs for housing and utilities are more than your gross monthly income and spendable resources combined.
- Your household's gross income and resources are below certain limits.

A worker will go over the forms with you in an interview. This may occur on the day you apply or at a later date. The eligibility worker will ask you for certain information such as bills, pay stubs, and rent receipts to prove your income and identify yourself. If you do not have the information that is requested, ask for a written list of additional information needed. Ask how many days you have to provide the information. The eligibility worker will answer questions and verify information. They cannot contact people outside your family (neighbors, employer, school) without your permission.

If your application is denied, you will be notified in writing. If you are approved, you will be sent a notice of approval and an identification card, showing how long the card is good and how many food stamps you will get.

The law now requires that a driver's license or an identification card be shown when food stamps are redeemed.

You will have to reapply before the end of your certification period. You will receive a form which will tell you the date by which you must reapply to continue to receive food stamps.

Supplemental Food Program for Women, Infants, and Children (WIC)

WIC is a federal program which provides extra food for pregnant women, new mother, infants, and young children who cannot afford an adequate diet. The WIC program provides nutritious food supplements to pregnant, breast-feeding and postpartum women, as well as to infants and children up to their fifth birthday.

In order to qualify, mother and children must be at medical or nutritional risk because of dietary need and inadequate income. Most WIC offices will give the mother a voucher that she can exchange for certain items at an approved grocery store. Many teen mothers qualify for and receive foods through WIC.

WIC offices are usually associated with health clinics, hospitals, and community centers that provide baby and maternity care. Some doctors and clinics refer patients in need to the program, but often families must find out about it and contact a WIC office on their own.

To be eligible, the mother or child must have a condition which shows a need for better nutrition. To determine this, simple tests are used such as measuring the baby's size or checking the iron level in the mother's blood. A test may not even be necessary, if the mother or child already qualifies because of something in her or his medical history.

Regrettably, because of a lack of funding, not everyone who is eligible for WIC receives benefits. The following is the priority list to reach those most in need:

- Pregnant or breast-feeding women.
- Infants up to 6 months of age or mothers at medical risk.

- Children up to age 5 at nutritional risk.
- Women who have recently given birth.

Each month, teen mothers pick up packets of food vouchers at a WIC site. The vouchers may be used at grocery stores to buy milk, cheese, eggs, juice, cereals, beans, and peanut butter. For infants, vouchers are available for iron-fortified infant formulas and cereals.

WIC participants also have the opportunity to learn more about good nutrition during pregnancy and while breast-feeding. They can share their concerns about breast-feeding and their children's eating habits with a counselor and other mothers involved in the program.

SUMMARY

You can buy food with government coupons called food stamps. Most teen parents have to spend cash as well as their food stamps in order to have enough food. You may apply for food stamps at your county welfare office. Households receiving AFDC are automatically eligible for food stamps. All other applicants must meet certain limits on money and property.

WIC (Women, Infants, and Children) provides extra food for pregnant women, new mothers, infants, and young children who cannot afford an adequate diet. In order to qualify, mothers and children must be at medical or nutritional risk due to dietary need and inadequate income. The mother will usually receive a voucher which she can exchange for certain items at an approved grocery store.

Issues for Teen Parents:

- Why are food stamps and WIC very helpful to teen parents?
- Where do you apply for these services?
- Who is eligible for food stamps and WIC?

Chapter VII

Medicaid is a government assistance program that pays the medical bills for low-income people who are unable to pay for medical care. Medicaid requires applicants to prove their financial need to be eligible. Many teen mothers do not seek medical care in the early months of pregnancy even though it may be available to them. States, however, must provide medicaid coverage to eligible, pregnant women once a doctor has confirmed pregnancy.

This chapter will:

- Describe how medicaid helps teenage parents.
- Help you understand the application process and health services that are covered.

Medicaid and Health Services

Some state have a medicaid program that covers "medically needy" individuals who would qualify for AFDC except for excessive income. Because of the high medical risk involved in teen pregnancies, some pregnant teens may be eligible for medicaid even if their parents' incomes are counted. The current federal law requires that all children in the AFDC programs be covered under the medicaid program.

States must provide medicaid coverage to the following:

- Individuals receiving AFDC.
- Pregnant women who are financially eligible for welfare but do not qualify for other reasons.
- Other groups and individuals who qualify.

Thus, if you are a teenage mother living with your parents and not eligible for welfare, you and the baby may be entitled to medicaid. Medicaid is important in bringing prenatal care to needy, pregnant adolescents. It should be noted that a baby may be eligible for medicaid even if the teen mother and the rest of the family are not.

Under the medicaid program, all states are required to offer the following to those who qualify:

- Inpatient and outpatient hospital services.
- Early Periodic Screening, Diagnosis, and Treatment (EPSDT).
- Family planning services.
- Physician services.

EPSDT can be a crucial input on the health of a low-income child. Under the program, examinations check on the child's growth and development, hearing, vision, and dental health; provide immunization; and identify and treat diseases and conditions such as tuberculosis, venereal disease, anemia or sickle-cell anemia, parasites, lead poisoning, and drug abuse.

It is important for young parents to understand that EPSDT provides periodic assessments for low-income children which would not necessarily otherwise be available under medicaid. Any adolescent who is medicaid eligible might be able to obtain important services, in addition to screening under the medicaid program.

Application Process

The teenager or the family may initiate the application process. Under the current regulations, a minor under 21 can apply for medicaid. The teen's parents will be contacted by medicaid to obtain financial information. If there is a failure to cooperate by the minor's parents or another legally responsible relative, medicaid can determine eligibility based on the income and resource information provided by the teen parent. Sometimes medicaid may have a special phone number for teen parents to call.

If you do not receive your own medicaid card, you should at least know your family's medicaid number. You may use your medicaid card like a credit card at any medical- or health-care provider that accepts medicaid. Make sure you ask first if they accept medicaid. You pay no money to the health-care provider; medicaid pays the bills directly.

What Health Services Are Covered?

In general, the following services are covered, although there may be some restrictions:

- Hospital inpatient and outpatient services.
- Laboratory and X-ray services.
- Care in a skilled nursing facility.
- Care in an intermediate care facility (health-related facility).
- Care through home health agencies.
- Treatment and preventive health care by physicians and dentists.
- Podiatrists.
- Eye care.
- Hearing aids.
- Treatment in psychiatric hospitals (for persons under 21 and over 64 years of age), mental health facilities, and mental retardation and developmental disabilities facilities.

- Family planning service.
- Early periodic screening, diagnosis, and treatment for children under 21 years of age.
- Drugs, supplies, equipment, and appliances (wheelchairs, etc.)
- Clinic services.
- Physical, occupation, and speech therapy.
- Audiology services.
- Private duty nursing.
- Clinical psychological services.
- Home health personal care services.
- Assurance of transportation to medicaid-covered medical services.

Medi-Cal

Medi-Cal is California's program to pay for medical care for recipients of public assistance and for other low-income persons. If you are receiving AFDC, you are automatically eligible for Medi-Cal. You may also qualify for Medi-Cal if you are under age 21, pregnant, or taking care of a child when one parent is employed or absent from the home.

You may apply for Medi-Cal by going to your county welfare office. If you are in a hospital ask the social worker to help you apply. If an emergency arises, it is possible to receive coverage the same day you apply. Be sure to tell the worker when an emergency application is needed.

The Child/Teen Health Plan

There may also be a child/teen health plan which is available *at no cost to you,* through your medicaid coverage. To qualify for the plan you simply have to be medicaid eligible and up through 20 years of age.

It is a preventative plan—the kind that keeps children and teens well and uncovers problems *before* they become serious. This health plan covers all medical needs:

- You get a medical exam and, if problems are found, follow-up treatment.
- Other services available include: pregnancy prevention, prenatal care, VD tests and treatment, alcohol and drug counseling, and help with personal problems.
- All services are confidential.
- Dental needs including yearly visits to the dentist for check-ups and cleaning.

If you are already getting these kinds of services, GREAT. KEEP IT UP! But if you would like help getting special health plan services for teens, call or stop in at your local department of social services.

What Is Prenatal Care?

Prenatal care falls into three areas: medical, nutritional, and social support for pregnant women. The medical part includes physical examinations, laboratory tests, and consultations with doctors and nurses to find and manage any problems that could injure the mother.

Women who receive medical care at the clinics are enrolled in the federal Special Supplemental Food Program for Women, Infants, and Children (WIC).

In prenatal care programs women learn how to take care of themselves and their newborns. They learn why they should exercise and why they should avoid drugs and cigarettes while they are pregnant.

Donna

Donna was pregnant at 16. She did not go to a clinic for prenatal care until the seventh month of her pregnancy. Because she was a teen mother with low income receiving late prenatal care, she was considered a high-risk birth case.

But Donna joined a prenatal group with other teen mothers, and they gave her the support she needed. She learned what delivery would be like and received helpful lessons in parenting. She got good advice from other young mothers in the program.

Now she has a healthy baby and some new friends at the clinic. Donna is glad she didn't listen to some of her friends who told her, "Prenatal care is a hassle" and that she would have transportation and child-care problems for her first child.

"For me," Donna said, "these programs were the beginning of a healthier, happier pregnancy and birth."

Homeless Teen Families

Homeless teen parents should not be afraid to contact the county because they think their children will be taken away from them. It is against the law for any government agency to take children away from their homeless parents unless there is evidence of abuse or neglect.

Homeless teen families may be eligible for special benefits to help them cope with "sudden and unusual circumstances beyond the family's control." This money can help homeless families get temporary shelter or rent and replace clothing and household items.

You may be immediately eligible for emergency assistance or money to spend on essentials such as medicine, transportation, and clothing.

SUMMARY

Medicaid is a government program that pays the medical bills for low-income people. States must provide medicaid coverage to eligible, pregnant women once a doctor has confirmed pregnancy. Under the current federal laws all children in AFDC programs are covered under the medicaid program.

Medicaid is important in bringing prenatal care to needy, pregnant young mothers. It provides inpatient and outpatient hospital services, early screening and diagnostic treatment, family planning services and doctor's services, and much, much more.

Medi-Cal is California's program to pay for medical care for both public assistance recipients and other low-income persons. If you are receiving AFDC you are automatically eligible for Medi-Cal. You may also qualify if you are under age 21, pregnant, or taking care of a child when one parent is unemployed or absent from the home.

Issues for Teen Parents:

- Why is it important for teen parents to have health insurance such as medicaid?
- What are the health-care services that teen parents have in your state?

CHAPTER VIII

Remember, if you are a teenage parent you are not alone. There are many organizations that can help you to obtain social services, acquire independent living skills, and protect and enforce your legal rights. Don't forget, however, that other people have legal rights, too: your family, your caseworker, your teachers, and others. All people have basic rights which you must respect. You do not have the right to break the law or hurt others. At the same time, these people should respect your rights.

This chapter will:

- Examine why the courts may appoint a guardian for a teen parent.
- Discuss why a man named the father of a child may need a lawyer.
- Name several individuals and agencies in your community who can assist you in protecting and enforcing your legal rights.

The Law and Teen Parents

In most states the age at which you are considered an adult is 18. Many teenage mother and fathers are minors—they have not yet reached their 18th birthday. Under the law, a minor is not regarded as legally competent with respect to legal matters. In many cases the courts will appoint a guardian for the minor parents to protect their rights. This guardian may be a parent, a lawyer, or another party. If the legal issues involve a possible conflict of interest between the parent and child, that parent will not be appointed guardian.

Depending on where you live, how young parents are handled by the courts varies greatly. Some courts believe that you are entitled to the protection of a guardian, a lawyer, or both. Many paternity defendants may not have legal counsel. If you are a defendant in a paternity case, you may need a guardian and legal assistance. You should also seek advice from knowledgeable friends or community leaders. A guardian and a lawyer are important because you may not understand the seriousness of your parental obligation. What you say and do will determine whether you are named the father of the child and ordered by the court to support the child for 18 years.

Another issue is statutory rape. Even if the young woman consents, sexual activity is a criminal offense if she is below a certain age. It is important to understand that minor parents have no lesser legal obligations to support their children than do parents who have reached the age of 18. Regrettably, many young parents are easily intimidated because of their age and inexperience. You may be required to appear at the child support and welfare offices to provide verbal and written information. You may have to appear as a witness and provide testimony in court. Many teen parents don't understand how to protect their rights. They are scared that if they don't do exactly as they are told, they will lose social service benefits and get in trouble.

GOING TO SCHOOL:
If You Have Children or Are Pregnant, You Have Rights!

You have a right to go to school. Your education must be free of charge. You have a right to go to school in the district where you live. You have a right to go to school even if you are pregnant or have children. You have a right to continue in your regular classroom and continue with your regular school activities. Your school cannot force you to attend special classes for pregnant students or students with children. If you want to stay in your regular classroom, you can!

Many schools have a special program for pregnant students or students with children. A teen mother may choose to be in this special program. Many of these alternative schools offer the following features:

Teen Parent Curriculum

- Complete curriculum appropriate for grade level:

English	Parenting
Math	Business skills
Health	Child development
Social studies	Adaptive physical education

- Infant child care
- A caring, supportive atmosphere
- Prenatal supervision by school nurse
- Nutritional information and education
- Labor and delivery instruction
- Counseling
- Pregnancy physiology
- Hot lunch program
- Maternity clothes closet

Many pregnant or parenting girls need the services offered by alternative high schools. These teen parenting schools pay special attention to your individual needs. Also, it is helpful to be with other pregnant girls at this time. You will find that you are not alone. You will have friends with whom you can share your feelings and concerns. In the teen parenting program, you should receive as good an education as your regular classroom would give you. In your special classrooms, you must be taught as much as your regular teachers would teach you. You must have good books and materials.

You cannot be forced to transfer to another school if you do not want to go. If the school plans to transfer you to another school, you have the right to ask the principal or superintendent to review the transfer. You may even ask for a fair hearing so that an impartial judge can review the transfer. **You have rights!**

THREE THINGS TO REMEMBER:

- The law prevents a school from making rules relating to the student's marital status, pregnancy, or parenthood.
- A school may not discriminate against or exclude any person because of pregnancy or childbirth.
- Disabilities related to pregnancy and childbirth must be treated the same as any other temporary disability or physical condition. If a doctor requires a student to be absent for a long period of time due to her pregnancy or childbirth, the school must allow such leave, and the student must be reinstated to the status she had before the leave began.

Schools for Pregnant Teens and Teen Parents

Teen parenting programs, or alternative schools, often have smaller classes than regular schools. Generally, they offer additional social services and special courses in parenting, health, and nutrition. In some schools, on-site day care is provided. Quite often these schools are a good choice for the young teen parent who may feel uncomfortable in the regular school.

If a pregnant teen or teen parent decides that she would like to attend a school for teenage parents, she may want to contact her counselor at the regular school, who will help her with the necessary paperwork. To register at the alternative school you may need a transcript of your schoolwork, a transfer request, and a doctor's certificate confirming your pregnancy. Your parents or guardian may be required to meet with the guidance counselor at your regular high school or new school.

Often the teen parenting school will make arrangements for the young mother to receive independent study work to complete at home. This will help her to keep up with her courses in the last weeks of her pregnancy and just after delivery. As long as the young mother's health is good, she may continue to attend classes.

Legal Assistance Programs and Teenage Parents

Many counties have legal assistance programs that provide free legal services for individuals under age 21 who are pregnant or have children. They may provide legal counsel and advice and represent you in court.

Some of these legal aid programs work closely with community agencies to teach pregnant and parenting minors their rights. In some counties, the legal aid office may help minor parents with the following:

- Legal problems regarding welfare, food stamps, and WIC.
- Rights to a free, quality education.
- Rights to health care.

Your legal aid office may provide help in many areas:

- **Housing:** Help you to obtain affordable housing and protect your rights against eviction.
- **Welfare:** AFDC, food stamps, and emergency services.
- **Family:** Paternity, custody, adoption, visitation, divorce, child support, foster care, day care, and independent living.
- **Health care:** Medicaid, hospital admissions, and medical treatment of minors and children.
- **Consumer:** Bill collections, contracts, loans, and obtaining credit.
- **Employment:** Job discrimination, wage claims, and unemployment insurance benefits.

You may be eligible for free legal assistance if you are under 21 years of age, have little or no income, and are either a father or a mother or are pregnant.

Emancipation of Minors

Emancipation of minors generally means the act of taking on the responsibilities and privileges of being an adult before reaching the age of 18 and not earlier than 14 years of age. There are many reasons why young parents may seek emancipation—for example:

- To have their own apartment or residence in their own name.
- To acquire a work permit without permission of the parents.

- To lessen parental control or interference.

There are several ways of becoming emancipated:

- By having a legal marriage.
- By being on active duty with any of the armed forces.
- By receiving a declaration of emancipation from the courts. This may require the minor parents to show the following:

    - That you are at least 14 years of age.
    - That you are living separately from your parents with either their consent or their knowledge.
    - That you are managing your own financial affairs.
    - That your income is not from illegal activities.

    (Many judges do not consider income from welfare or other state assistance as being financially self-sufficient.)

In your county, there may not be a procedure for becoming emancipated. If you are living away from home and are self-supporting, you may be considered emancipated. Many counties, however, will have other legal requirements. If you are emancipated, you may qualify for welfare and medicaid benefits without your parents' permission.

The following are individuals and agencies who may be able to assist you in protecting and enforcing your legal rights:

    Caseworker
    Community leaders
    Counselor
    Emergency services
    Family/clinic doctor
    Family court
    Hospital parenting program
    Lawyer
    Legal aid
    Minister, Priest, Rabbi
    Parents/guardian
    Police
    Responsible friends
    Teachers
    Teen parenting program

SUMMARY

As teenage parents you have legal rights regarding school, housing, social services, health care, employment, paternity, custody, visitation, child support, and adoption.

When you need help you should check with the legal assistance program in your community. They may provide free legal services for individuals under age 21 who are pregnant or have children. They also may provide legal counsel and advice and represent you in court.

Issues for Teen Parents:

- What kind of legal problems do teen parents in your community have regarding paternity, custody, child support, and visitation?
- What legal rights does a "father" have to custody and visitation if paternity has not been established?
- What are the laws in your state regarding a minor father voluntarily admitting paternity?
- What are the rights of teen parents to complete their education when they are pregnant or parenting?
- How is a teen parenting program different from a regular school environment?
- How can legal assistance help teen parents? Where do you apply for legal assistance in your community?
- Do you know any teen parents who are emancipated? What are the pros and cons of emancipation?

Chapter IX

It is important that you stay in school! Many young parents drop out of school and never complete their high school education. They are often forced to depend on public assistance until they can acquire the education and job skills to enable them to become independent and self-sufficient. Teen mothers and fathers who stay in school have a much better chance of getting a good job. If you have already dropped out of school, you should talk to counselors about returning to school. You have a right to an education.

This chapter will:

- Describe the importance of school and job training.
- Describe the types of information teen parents are asked to provide when applying for a job.

Stay in School

It may take time to be a parent and go to school. It won't be easy. You will have to pull all your resources together—body, mind, and spirit. If you really want it, you have to work for it. You must make it happen. Go out and get it! It will take character and strength. You may not get encouragement from your friends and relatives. You must assume personal responsibility for your future. In this process you are getting to know who you really are.

You may have friends who quit school and went on public assistance with no plans for getting off. Not only your future is at stake, but also your child's. If you want money to survive and a decent job, getting a high school diploma or some kind of job training is an absolute necessity.

If you are over 16, you can get a high school diploma by studying for a Graduate Equivalency Dilpoma (GED). A GED means that you have had the same training as a high school graduate. You may want to contact a high school or job training center to find out more about this.

After you have completed high school, you should be setting new goals. You may choose to go to a trade school, business school, or college. You may want to get a job or join the military. You may want to get married or enroll in a job training program.

JOB TRAINING HELPS!

Many teen parents have so many problems that they have little time or resources to think about employment. Yet this is a very important concern for teen parents. Many communities have programs that offer training and work experience to teen parents. You should talk with a counselor or community leader about these programs.

Studies have shown that many teen parents who enroll in programs to train them for jobs and help them become better parents go on to earn higher salaries than teen parents who do not receive this help.

Many of these programs had a major impact on teenagers who were receiving welfare when they began the program. Many of the young parents who completed the program had found jobs and were earning a good income. The job programs for young parents can help to reduce the chances of long-term welfare dependency and poverty.

Getting a Job

Many teenage parents have a part-time job after school or on weekends. Having a part-time job helps you not only to earn money but also to find out what kind of work you enjoy. When you apply for a job, you will be asked your social security number, home address, and date of birth. You may be asked the name of all your schools and the dates you attended. You will also be asked to list where you've worked and any school activities. In addition, the employer may ask for the names, addresses, and phone numbers of three people who would recommend you.

You may have a job interview. You should dress well and not chew gum or smoke. Do not use slang or street language. Be polite and listen carefully during the interview. You may be asked why you want the job and what your plans are for the future.

Job Discrimination

If you believe that you have been discriminated against in hiring based on sex, race, age, religion, or handicap, you should contact the Commission of Human Rights in your community. If you believe that your employer is not paying you what you've earned, you should contact him and try to settle the matter. If you still have problems, you may contact the Wages and Hours Division of the Department of Labor.

SUMMARY

Stay in school! Many young parents drop out of school and never complete their education. Teenage parents who stay in school have a better chance of getting a good job.

It's not easy to be a full-time parent and student. It takes real character and strength. You are making short-term sacrifices for yourself and your child. By choosing to stay in school, you are taking personal responsibility for your family's future.

Issues for Teen Parents:

- Are there job training programs for teen parents in your community? How have they helped teen parents?
- Despite their difficult schedule, many teen parents will have a part-time job. What do you feel are the pros and cons of having a part-time job after school or on weekends?

Chapter X

Many teenagers are responsible parents, and we are proud to describe this positive side of teen parenting. We are not, however, encouraging teenagers to become parents. Most teenagers can accomplish a great deal by waiting to become parents. For those who are teen parents, our goal is to help you become the best parents possible.

This chapter will:

- Help you understand how teen parents are making decisions and solving problems.

Teen Parents Who Are Taking Responsibility

The following are the stories of real teen parents. Many of them are in situations where they have to be responsible under extremely difficult circumstances. Many of them have to overcome several obstacles and disadvantages in achieving their goals. They show the courage, determination, and commitment it takes to become independent and build a good life for their family.

LINDA, 17, unmarried

Linda is a responsible and caring mother. It's not easy. She must take care of herself because her parents are deceased. She attends a vocational school and works part-time at a fast-food outlet. With the help of her teen program and the "Y," Linda is working hard to be a good mother for her child.

At first Linda quit school and went on welfare. "All I did every day was sit home and watch soap operas and quiz shows. It was a dead end. I knew that somehow I had to go back to school. My baby was born with medical problems, and I have to take her to the hospital each week. It's not easy, but I'm doing it."

MELVIN, 17, unmarried

Many teenage parents are proud to be parents. One teenage parent, Melvin, has an 18-month old baby. "I get him a few hours on the weekend, and my aunt helps me watch him. I have a part-time job after school and go over to see him whenever I can. Sometimes I bring baby food and Pampers to help out. The baby's mother is dating someone else, but she still wants me to be with my child. I admitted in court that I was the father. I don't drink, hang out, or do drugs. I work hard and am going to school. No one can ever say I ran out on my son."

DELORES, 16, and WILBUR, 17
married

For Wilbur and Delores it is a happier story. They both give love and support to their child. Delores's parents asked Wilbur to move into their house so that he could be closer to the child and mother. Wilbur enjoys holding the baby and taking care of her. They are hoping to get an apartment when they finish high school. "It's not easy, but we are working hard to make our dreams come true."

EVE, 16, unmarried

"I'm going to have a baby. I need health care. I am going to need welfare and food stamps to live on until I get out of high school and find a job. I need to go to court to name the father of the child and apply for child support. I need child care services so I can stay in school. In other words, I have to make tough decisions so that my baby and me can survive and get on in this world."

SUSAN, 16, and JOSÉ, 17, unmarried

Susan attends a teen parenting school in California. She also participates in the adolescent parenting program at the medical center. She meets with a social worker on a regular basis for counseling and during her pregnancy receives prenatal care at a local center. She has the opportunity to share her feelings, problems, and concerns with her friends in the teen parenting programs. José, the father of the child, also participates in these programs. Susan is completing her high school education, acquiring job skills, and learning about parenting, nutrition, and her legal rights.

Susan has learned how to juggle her schedule to meet the demands of a full-time mother and full-time student. She realizes that if she had more children right now it would not help her and the baby toward becoming independent and self-sufficient.

Susan is looking forward to becoming a keypunch operator upon graduation. José is planning to work at an auto body shop and attend community college in the evenings. They have control over their lives and are working hard to build a good future for themselves and their child.

SUMMARY

Many teen parents are learning to make responsible decisions regarding their medical and child care needs. They are able to deal with the problems of paternity, child support, custody, and visitation. These teen parents are able to interact with social services, courts, and community agencies. These young parents love their children and want the best for them. They are working hard to build a good future for themselves and their family. They have learned how to build a support network and protect their legal rights as they become independent and self-supporting.

Issues for Teen Parents:

- Why are some teen parents able to cope with their problems better than others?
- How effective is your support network?

GLOSSARY

Absent Parent — Any individual who is absent from the home and is legally responsible for providing financial support for a dependent child.

Aid — Aid to Families with Dependent Children, emergency assistance, or AFDC/foster care.

Aid to Families with Dependent Chidren — A category of public assistance (welfare). The term *welfare* involves three programs: Aid to Families with Dependent Children (AFDC), medicaid, and food stamps. The welfare program is a large source of public support for teenage mothers and their children.

Alleged Father — A person who has been named as the father of a child born out of wedlock but for whom paternity has not been established.

Assistance — Support money or goods granted to a person or family based on income.

Blood Testing — Helps to minimize the guesswork involved in determining the father of a child. They can show either that the man is definitely not the father or that he is probably the father.

Child care classes — Courses or other educational programs which teach about how to take care of a child and how to parent.

Child care services — Care by an adult other than parents for some part of each day while parents work, attend school, or are otherwise engaged. These services are also know as day care.

Child Support — The legal duty of parents to provide for their children.

Custody — Legal care and control of the children.

Dependent — A person to whom a duty of support is owed.

Due Process — The conduct of legal proceedings according to those rules and principles that have been established in our system of law for the enforcement and protection of civil rights.

Emancipation — The act of taking on the responsibilities and privileges of being an adult before reaching the age of 18.

Family Court — A court that is concerned with the needs of the family.

Food Stamps — Government coupons provided to increase the food purchasing power of low-income households to the point where they can purchase a low-cost diet that is nutritionally adequate.

GED — Graduate Equivalency Diploma. The GED exam is a standardized test for which a qualifying score earns an alternative certificate to the high school diploma. GED classes prepare in and out of school students in the subject ar. as assessed by the exam.

Good Cause The mother may have a good cause not to cooperate in identifying the father in a paternity action. That is, if cooperation may result in serious physical or emotional harm to the child or mother, the child was conceived as a result of incest or rape, or adoption proceedings are under way.

Guardian Many young unwed parents are not of the age of majority (in most states that age is 18). They must have someone of legal age to help protect their legal rights. This may be a parent or another party appointed by the court. A guardian is responsible for making decisions and controlling your legal interests.

JTPA The Federal Job Training Partnership Act of 1982 establishes programs to prepare youth and unskilled adults for entry into the labor force and to afford job training to economically disadvantaged individuals and others facing serious barriers to employment. Pregnant or parenting teenagers are considered to have a barrier to employment that qualifies them for JTPA services regardless of whether they meet other economic requirements. JTPA replaces CETA, the Comprehensive Employment and Training Act.

Judge Conducts legal proceedings according to those rules and principles that have been established for the enforcement and protection of civil rights. The judge will listen to your story. He makes the decisions: whom the child will live with, who is the father of the child. Also, the judge decides visitation rights and child support.

Legal Father A man who is recognized by law as the male parent of another person.

Low birth weight Describes infants born weighing less than or equal to 2500 grams or 5-1/2 pounds. Due to the low weight, these infants are considered high risk for disease or mortality.

Medicaid A government assistance program that pays the medical bills for low-income people who are unable to pay for medical care. States must provide medicaid coverage to eligible pregnant women once a doctor has confirmed the pregnancy.

Paternity The legal establishment of father-child relationship.

Paternity Case An action to determine the father of a child born out of wedlock.

Prenatal care Medical and health care during pregnancy.

Public Assistance Support money or goods granted to a person or family based on income.

Putative Father Alleged father. A person who has been named as the father of a child born out of wedlock but for whom paternity has not been established.

Statutory Rape	Having sexual intercourse with a woman under a certain age (usually 16), even if both parties consent.
Visitation Agreement	As part of a court order, it defines the rights of the noncustodial party to be with the child.
Well-child clinic	A clinic that provides services to children that are not necessarily ill from a suspected disease, but are in need of vaccinations, physical exams, and other preventive measures to ensure that the child is developing properly and stays well.
WIC	The Special Supplemental Food Program for Women, Infants, and Children providing vitamins, nutritious foods, and health care for pregnant women, lactating mothers, infants, and children.

EXHIBIT I

SAMPLE - BLOOD TEST ORDER

IN THE DISTRICT COURT OF THE STATE OF IOWA

IN AND FOR _____ COUNTY _____

STATE OF IOWA, EX. REL.,

_____
Complainant,

vs.

_____
Defendant.

NO. _____

STIPULATION REGARDING
BLOOD TEST

COME NOW the parties to this action and here by stipulate and agree to the following:

1. The parties will present themselves, and Complainant will present the child for whom a paternity adjudication is being sought herein, at a time and place to be arranged for the purpose of drawing blood samples.
2. Said blood samples shall be forwarded to the Minneapolis Memorial Blood Bank for analysis to determine whether or not Defendant could be the father of the child named in the Paternity Complaint.
3. Defendant shall pay all of costs of blood analysis.
4. Test results shall be furnished to both parties as soon as available.
5. If said analysis shall exclude Defendant from being a possible father of the child, then this action shall be dismissed.
6. Neither party will challenge the chain of custody of the book samples, and the test results may be offered as evidence and admitted without objection for whatever probative value they have.
7. If the test results are disputed, the Court, upon reasonable request of either party, may order additional testing at the expense of the requesting party.
8. In the event that he is not excluded as a possible father of the child in question, Defendant agrees:

Date: _____

Date: _____

_____
Attorney for Defendant

_____
Attorney for Complainant

EXHIBIT II
SAMPLE QUESTIONS FOR ALLEGED FATHER

PLEASE TAKE NOTICE that pursuant to Rule   of the   Rules of Civil Procedure, Plaintiff requests that the defendant answer the following interrogatories under oath. Such interrogatories shall be answered full and in writing.

1. Are you acquainted with the plaintiff?
2. If your answer is in the affirmative, please state when and where you first met her and fully describe the circumstances. Did you obtain her name, address, and telephone number?
3. How many times did you visit her?
4. Was anyone else present when you visited her, and if so, list the names of all persons present.
5. Did you ever live at the same address as the plaintiff?
6. Did you ever have sexual intercourse with the plaintiff? If "yes," answer the following:

    State the periods (whether day or night) during which sexual intercourse with the plaintiff occurred.

    State when, where, and how many times sex acts with the plaintiff took place.
7. Did you ever tell anyone that you had sexual intercourse or an affair with the plaintiff? If you did, list the names and addresses of such persons.
8. Did you claim that persons other than yourself engaged in sexual intercourse with the plaintiff? If so, please state the following for each such person:

    (a) Name(s) and address(es).

    (b) Date(s) and place(s) of each occurrence.

    (c) Whether or not you plan to call said person(s) as your witness(es).
9. Please state the names, addresses, and telephone numbers of all witnesses you know who may have information relevant to this case.
10. Please state your blood type, including RH factor.
11. At any time that you had sexual intercourse with the plaintiff did you use any birth control measures? Did she? If yes, state what measures were used by either or both of you.
12. Did you know that the plaintiff gave birth to a child on   ?
13. Did you ever tell any other person that you were the father of the child. If "yes," please state the names and addresses of all such persons to whom such statements have been made.
14. If you specifically deny that you are the father of the plaintiff's child, please state in detail why you do not think you are the father.
15. Did you take or offer to take the plaintiff to the doctor or hospital for the delivery of her child?
16. Did you ever offer to marry the plaintiff?
17. Did you ever offer to pay toward the support of the plaintiff's child?
18. Do you carry any insurance? If so, state the name and address of the insurance company.

BIBLIOGRAPHY

Barret, R.L., and Robinson, B.E. "The Adolescent Father." In *Dimensions in Fatherhood*, edited by S.M. Hanson and R.W. Bozett. Beverly Hills, Calif.: Sage Publications, 1985.

Boocheever, S. *Improving Services to Young Parents through CETA*. Washington, D.C.: U.S. Department of Labor, Employment and Training Administration, Government Printing Office, 1980.

Bumpass, L.L., and Sweet, J.A., "Children and Marital Disruption: A Replication and Update." *Demography* 21 (1984), 71-82.

Bureau of the Census. *Child Support and Alimony: 1985*. Current Population Report, series P-23, no. 152. Washington, D.C.: U.S. Department of Commerce, 1987.

Burt, M. *Estimates of Public Costs for Teenage Childbearing*. Paper prepared for the Center for Population Options, Washington, D.C., 1986.

Burt, M.R., Kimmich, M.H., Goldmuntz, J., and Sonnenstein, F.L. *Helping Pregnant Adolescents: Outcomes and Costs of Service Delivery*. Washington, D.C.: Urban Institute, 1984.

California University, San Fransico Institute for Health Policy Studies, San Fransico Family Service Agency. *Teenage Pregnancy and Parenting Project: 1983-84 Annual Report and Evaluation*. Office of Adolescent Pregnancy Programs (PHS), Washington, D.C., 1985.

Card, J.J. *Inventory of Contents, Data Sources on Young Male Sexuality, Contraception, and Fatherhood as Found in the Data Archives on Adolescent Pregnancy and Pregnancy Prevention*. Palo Alto, Calif.: Sociometrics Corporation, 1986.

Cassetty, J., ed. *The Parental Child-Support Obligation*. Lexington, Mass.: Lexington Books, 1983.

Center for the Study of Social Policy. *Preventing Teenage Pregnancy: A Literature Review*. Washington, D.C.: Center for the Study of Social Policy, 1986.

Chambers, D.L. *Making Fathers Pay: The Enforcement of Child Support*. Chicago: University of Chicago Press, 1979.

Cherlin, A., Griffith, J., and McCarthy, J. "A Note on Maritally Disrupted Men's Reports of Child Support in 1980 Current Population Survey." *Demography* vol. 20, no. 3 (August 1983): 385-89.

Child Welfare League of America. *Substitute Care Programs for Young Mothers and Their Infants: An Overview*, p.70. Washington, D.C., 1984.

DeJong, W., et. al. *Adolescent Parenthood: Developing a Comprehensive Community Planning Guide around the Issue of Teenage Pregnancy*. Flint, Mich.: Mott Foundation, 1984.

Eldeman, M.W. *Families in Peril: An Agenda for Social Change.* Cambridge, Mass.: Harvard University Press, 1987.

Ellwood, D. *Targeting "Would-Be" Long-Term Recipients of AFDC.* Princeton, N.J.: Mathematica, 1986.

Furstenberg, F., Brookes-Gunn, J., and Morgan, S.P. *Adolescent Mothers in Later Life.* Cambridge, Mass.: Cambridge University Press, 1987.

Haskins, R., Dobelstein, A., Akin, J., and Schwartz, J. *Estimates of National Child Support Collections Potential and Income Security of Female-Headed Families.* Chapel Hill, Press: University of North Carolina 1985.

Hayes, C. *Risking the Future: Adolescent Sexuality, Pregnancy, and Childbearing.* Final Report on Adolescent Pregnancy and Childbearing, vol. 1, and Working Papers, vol. 2. Washington, D.C.: National Academy Press, 1987.

Horowitz, R.M., Dodson, D., and Haynes, M.C. *Remedies under the Child Support Enforcement Amendments of 1984.* Washington, D.C.: Office of Child Support Enforcement, Department of Health and Human Services, 1985.

Johnson, C., and Sum, A. *Declining Earnings of Young Men: Their Relation to Poverty, Teen Pregnancy, and Family Formation.* A Clearinghouse Report. Washington, D.C.: Children's Defense Fund, 1987.

Kirby, D. *School-Based Clinics: An Emerging Approach to Improving Adolescent Health and Addressing Teenage Pregnancy.* Washington, D.C.: Center for Population Options, 1985.

Lamb, M.E., and Elster, A., eds. *Adolescent Fatherhood.* Hillsdale, N.J.: Lawrence Erlbaum Associates, 1986.

Lamb, M.E., and Sagi, A., eds. *Fatherhood and Family Policy.* Hillsdale, N.J.: Lawrence Erlbaum Associates, 1983.

Lancaster, J.B., and Hamburg, B.A. *School Age Pregnancy and Parenthood: Bio-Social Dimensions.* New York: Aldine de Gruyper, 1986.

Lerman, Robert L. "A National Profile of Young Unwed Fathers: Who Are They and How Are They Parenting?" October 1986, unpublished.

Moore, K. *Facts at a Glance: An Update.* Washington, D.C.: Child Trends, 1986.

Moore, K. "Government Policies Related to Teenage Family Formation and Functioning: An Inventory." In *Teenage Pregnancy in a Family Context: Implication for Policy*, edited by T. Ooms. Philadelphia: Temple University Press, 1981.

Moore, K.A., and Burt, M.R. *Private Crisis, Public Cost: Policy Perspectives on Teenage Childbearing.* Washington, D.C.: Urban Institute Press, 1982.

National Urban League. *Adolescent Male Responsibility: Pregnancy Prevention and Parenting Program: A Program Development Guide.* A report of the Adolescent Male Responsibility Project. New York: National Urban League, 1987. [Includes brief profiles of 26 programs.]

Nickel, P., and Delaney, H. *Working with Teen Parents: A Survey of Promising Approaches.* Chicago: Family Resource Coalition, 1985.

Ooms, T., ed. *Teenage Pregnancy in a Family Context: Implications for Policy.* Philadelphia: Temple University Press, 1981.

Parke, R., and Neville, B. "Teenage Fatherhood." In *Risking the Future: Adolescent Sexuality, Pregnancy and Childbearing,* vol. 2. edited by Cheryl Hayes. Washington, D.C.: National Academy Press, 1987.

Pierce, W. *Adoption Factbook: United States Data, Issues, Regulations and Resources.* Washington, D.C.: National Committee for Adoption, 1985.

Pitman, K. *Adolescent Pregnancy: What the States Are Saying.* Clearinghouse Report no. 2. Washington, D.C.: Children's Defense Fund, 1986.

Pitman, K. *Adolescent Pregnancy: Whose Problem Is It?* Clearinghouse Report no. 1. Washington, D.C.: Children's Defense Fund, 1986.

Pritchard, M.L., Smith, T.J., and Thompson, C. *A Practitioner's Guide: Strategies, Programs, and Resources for Youth Employability Development.* Philadelphia: Public/Private Ventures, 1984.

Sander, J. *Working with Teenage Fathers: Handbook for Program Development.* New York: Bank Street College of Education, 1986. [Provides brief profiles of 5 program models.]

Scales, P., and Beckstein, D. "From Macho to Mutuality: Helping Young Men Make Effective Decisions About Sex, Contraception, and Pregnancy." In *Pregnancy in Adolescence: Needs, Problems, and Management,* edited by Stuart and Wells. New York: Van Nostrand Reinhold Company, 1982.

Select Committee of Children, Youth and Families. *Teen Pregnancy: What is Being Done? A State-by-State Look.* Washington, D.C.: U.S. Government Printing Office, 1986.

Wattenberg, Esther. "Protecting the Rights of the Minor Child of Unmarried Minor Parents: Toward a Rational Policy." Paper presented to the Child Support Enforcement Research Workshop, Office of Child Support Enforcement, U.S. Department of Health and Human Services, Washington, D.C., August 18, 1984. School of Social Work, Center for Urban and Regional Affairs, University of Minnesota (mimeo).

Young, Edward M. *Cost and Benefits of Paternity Establishment.* Pasadena, Calif.: Center for Health and Social Services Research, 1985.

STATE AGENCIES ADMINISTERING CHILD SUPPORT PROGRAMS UNDER TITLE IV-D OF THE SOCIAL SECURITY ACT

ALABAMA
Director
Bureau of Child Support
Alabama Department of Pensions
  and Security
64 North Union Street
Montgomery, Alabama 36130
(205) 261-2872

ALASKA
Director
Child Support Enforcement Division
Department of Revenue
4th Floor
550 West 7th Avenue
Anchorage, Alaska 99501
(907) 276-3441

ARIZONA
Administrator
Child Support Enforcement Administration
Department of Economic Security
P.O. Box 6123 - Site Code 776A
Phoenix, Arizona 85005
(602) 255-3465

ARKANSAS
Director
Office of Child Support Enforcement
Arkansas Social Services
P.O. Box 3358
Little Rock, Arkansas 72203
(501) 371-2464

CALIFORNIA
Chief
Child Support Program
  Management Branch
Department of Social Services
744 P Street
Sacramento, California 95814
(916) 323-8994

COLORADO
Director
Division of Child Support Enforcement
Department of Social Services
717 Seventeenth Street
P.O. Box 181000
Denver, Colorado 80218-0899
(303) 294-5994

CONNECTICUT
Director
Bureau of Child Support Enforcement
Department of Human Resources
1049 Asylum Avenue
Hartford, Connecticut 06105
(203) 566-3053

DELAWARE
Director
Division of Child Support Enforcement
Department of Health & Social Services
P.O. Box 904
New Castle, Delaware 19720
(302) 421-8300

DISTRICT OF COLUMBIA
Chief
Office of Paternity and Child Support
Department of Human Services
425 "I" Street, N.W., 3rd Floor
Washington, D.C. 20001
(202) 724-5610

FLORIDA
Director
Office of Child Support Enforcement
Department of Health
  & Rehabilitative Services
1317 Winewood Boulevard—Bldg. 3
Tallahassee, Florida 32399-0700
(904) 488-9900

GEORGIA
Director
Office of Child Support Recovery
State Department of Human Resources
P.O. Box 80000
Atlanta, Georgia 30357
(404) 894-4119

GUAM
Supervisor
Child Support Enforcement Office
Department of Public Health
  & Social Services
California First Bank Building
194 Hernan Cortez Avenue, 2nd Floor
Agana, Guam 96910
(617) 477-2036

HAWAII
Director
Child Support Enforcement Agency
Department of Attorney General
770 Kapiolani Boulevard—Suite 703
Honolulu, Hawaii 96813
(808) 548-5779

IDAHO
Bureau of Child Support Enforcement
Department of Health and Welfare
Statehouse Mail
Boise, Idaho 83720
(208) 334-5710

ILLINOIS
Chief
Bureau of Child Support Enforcement
Illinois Department of Public Aid
Jesse B. Harris Building
P.O. Box 2127
100 South Grand Avenue East
Springfield, Illinois 62705
(217) 782-1366

INDIANA
Director
Child Support Enforcement Division
Department of Public Welfare
4th Floor
141 South Meridian Street
Indianapolis, Indiana 46225
(317) 232-4885

IOWA
Chief
Bureau of Collections
Iowa Department of Human Services
Hoover Building—5th Floor
Des Moines, Iowa 50319
(515) 281-5580

KANSAS
Administrator
Child Support Enforcement Program
Department of Social &
 Rehabilitation Services
2700 West Sixth
1st Floor, Perry Building
Topeka, Kansas 66606
(913) 296-3237

KENTUCKY
Director
Division of Child Support Enforcement
Department of Social Insurance
Cabinet of Human Resources
275 East Main Street, 6th Floor East
Frankfort, Kentucky 40621
(502) 654-2285

LOUISIANA
Director
Support Enforcement Service Program
Office of Family Security
Department of Health and
 Human Resources
P.O. Box 94065
Baton Rouge, Louisiana 70804
(504) 342-4780

MAINE
Director
Support Enforcement and Location Unit
Bureau of Social Welfare
Department of Human Services
State House, Station II
Augusta, Maine 04333
(207) 289-2886

MARYLAND
Executive Director
Child Support Enforcement Administration
Department of Human Resources
Eleven East Mount Royal Avenue
Baltimore, Maryland 21201
(301) 333-3978

MASSACHUSETTS
Director
Child Support Enforcement Unit
Department of Revenue
100 Cambridge Street—Room 805
Boston, Massachusetts 02204
(617) 727-3950

MICHIGAN
Director
Office of Child Support
Department of Social Services
300 South Capitol Avenue—Suite 621
Lansing, Michigan 48909
(517) 373-7570

MINNESOTA
Director
Office of Child Support
Department of Human Services
Suite 403
Metro Square Building
St. Paul, Minnesota 55101
(612) 296-2499

MISSISSIPPI
Director
Child Support Division
State Department of Public Welfare
P.O. Box 352
515 E. Amite Street
Jackson, Mississippi 39205
(601) 354-0341, ext. 503

MISSOURI
Administrator
Child Support Enforcement Unit
Division of Legal Services
Department of Social Services
P.O. Box 1527
Jefferson City, Missouri 65102-1527
(314) 751-4301

MONTANA
Director
Child Support Enforcement Program
Department of Revenue
Investigation and Enforcement Division
P.O. Box 5955
Helena, Montana 59604
(406) 444-4614

NEBRASKA
Administrator
Child Support Enforcement Office
Department of Social Services
P.O. Box 95026
Lincoln, Nebraska 68509
(402) 471-9125

NEVADA
Chief
Child Support Enforcement Program
Department of Human Resources
2527 North Carson Street, Capital Complex
Carson City, Nevada 89710
(702) 885-4744

NEW HAMPSHIRE
Administrator
Office of Child Support
 Enforcement Services
Division of Welfare
Health and Welfare Building
Hazen Drive
Concord, New Hampshire 03301
(603) 271-4426

NEW JERSEY
Director
New Jersey Division of Public Welfare
Bureau of Child Support & Paternity Unit
CN 716
Trenton, New Jersey 08625
(609) 588-2401

NEW MEXICO
Chief
Child Support Enforcement Bureau
Department of Human Services
P.O. Box 2348—PERA Building
Santa Fe, New Mexico 87503
(505) 827-4230

NEW YORK
Director
Office of Child Support Enforcement
New York State Department of
 Social Services
P.O. Box 14
1 Commerce Plaza
Albany, New York 12260
(518) 474-9081

NORTH CAROLINA
Chief
Child Support Enforcement Section
Division of Social Services
Department of Human Resources
433 N. Harrington Street
Raleigh, North Carolina 27603-1393
(919) 733-4120

NORTH DAKOTA
Administrator
Child Support Enforcement Agency
North Dakota Department of
 Human Services
State Capitol
Bismarck, North Dakota 58505
(701) 224-3582

OHIO
Chief
Bureau of Child Support
Ohio Department of Human Services
State Office Tower
30 East Broad Street—27th Floor
Columbus, Ohio 43215
(614) 466-3233

OKLAHOMA
Administrator
Attention: Division of Child Support
Department of Human Services
P.O. Box 25352
Oklahoma City, Oklahoma 73125
(405) 424-5871

OREGON
Director
Recovery Services Section
Adult and Family Services Division
Department of Human Resources
P.O. Box 14506
Salem, Oregon 97309
(503)378-5439

PENNSYLVANIA
Director
Child Support Programs
Bureau of Claim Settlement
Department of Public Welfare
P.O. Box 8018
Harrisburg, Pennsylvania 17105
(717) 783-5184

PUERTO RICO
Director
Child Support Enforcement Program
Department of Social Services
CALL Box 3349
San Juan, Puerto Rico 00904
(809) 722-4731

RHODE ISLAND
Chief Supervisor
Bureau of Family Support
Department of Social &
 Rehabilitative Services
77 Dorance Street
Providence, Rhode Island 02903
(401) 277-2409

SOUTH CAROLINA
Director
Child Support Enforcement Division
Department of Social Services
P.O. Box 1520
Columbia, South Carolina 29202-9988
(803) 737-9938

SOUTH DAKOTA
Program Administrator
Office of Child Support Enforcement
Department of Social Services
700 Governors Drive
Pierre, South Dakota 57501-2291
(605) 773-3641

TENNESSEE
Director
Child Support Services
Department of Human Services
Citizens Plaza Building—12th Floor
400 Deadrick Street
Nashville, Tennessee 37219
(615) 741-1820

TEXAS
Director
Child Support Enforcement Division
c/o Attorney General's Office
P.O. Box 12548
Austin, Texas 78711-2548
(512) 463-2181

UTAH
Director
Office of Recovery Services
Department of Social Services
120 North—200 West
P.O. Box 45011
Salt Lake City, Utah 84145-0011
(801) 538-4400

VERMONT
Director
Child Support Division
Department of Social Welfare
103 South Main Street
Waterbury, Vermont 05676
(802) 241-2868

VIRGIN ISLANDS
Director
Support and Paternity Division
Department of Law
46 Norre Gade
St. Thomas, Virgin Islands 00801
(809) 776-0372

VIRGINIA
Director
Division of Support Enforcement Program
Department of Social Services
8004 Franklin Farms Drive
Richmond, Virginia 23288
(804) 281-9297

WASHINGTON
Chief
Office of Support Enforcement
Department of Social & Health Services
P.O. Box 9162-FU-11
Olympia, Washington 98504
(206) 459-6481

WEST VIRGINIA
Director
Office of Child Support Enforcement
Department of Human Services
1900 Washington Street, East
Charleston, West Virginia 25305
(304) 348-3780

WISCONSIN
Director
Division of Community Services
Office of Child Support
1 West Wilson Street, Room 385
P.O. Box 7851
Madison, Wisconsin 53707-7851
(608) 266-9909

WYOMING
Director
Child Support Enforcement Section
Div. of Public Assistance & Social Services
State Dept. of Health & Social Services
Hathaway Building
Cheyenne, Wyoming 82002
(307) 777-7892

INDEX

AFDC (welfare):
   appeal, 83
   applying for, 75, 79-80
   college students, 86
   eligibility, 73-76
   Family Welfare Reform Act, 76
   fathers, 85
   grant, 77
   good cause, 82
   interview, 78
   policies, 74
   problems, 73
   tips, 84
   work requirements, 85
Birth certificate, 40-41
Blood tests, 32-33
Child care:
   need for, 27-28
   evaluating, 28
Child support:
   amount of support,
   custody and visitation, 64-65
   enforcing your order, 65-66
   going to court, 61
   grandparents, 66
   how much support, 58
   information checklist, 60
   order of protection, 63
   public assistance, 59
   services provided, 54
Court: court order, 65-66
   going to court, 61-63
Custody, 64
Emancipation, 109-111
Emergency assistance, 26
Family courts: definition, 57
   preparing your case, 59-60
Fathers: guidelines, 19-21
   needs, 18-19
   paternity, 33-34, 36-37
   visitation, 65
   welfare, 85
Food stamps, application, 89
   definition, 88
Graduate Equivalency Diploma (GED), 114
Guardian, 103-104
Homeless teen families, 100
Health care, see Medicaid/Medi-Cal
Hospitals: parenting programs, 29
   prenatal care, 99
   resources, 29
Job training: discrimination, 116
   need for, 115
Judge: role of,
Law: emancipation, 109
   guardian, 104
   legal assistance, 108

   paternity, 31-34
   rights of teen parents, 103-105
   school, 105-107
   statutory rape, 105
   teen parent curriculum, 106
Medicaid/Medi-Cal: application, 96-97
   child teen plan, 99
   definition, 94
   eligibility, 95
   EPSDT, 96
   Medi-Cal, 98
   prenatal care, 99-100
   services covered, 97-98
Mothers: needs of, 13-16
Order of protection, 63
Paternity: benefits, 38-40
   blood testing, 33
   birth certificate, 40-41
   definition, 31
   flier, 43-44
   good cause,
   interview, 41-42, Exhibit II
   lawyer, 33
   unwed mothers, 34-35
   unwed fathers, 36
   voluntary acknowledgment, 34
Prenatal care 99-100
Resource directory: child care, 27-28
   emergency assistance, 26
   parenting programs, 29
Schools: for teen parents, 107
   staying in school, 113
Statutory rape, 105
Teen parents:
   child support, 53-70
   fathers, 17-20
   food stamps, 88-92
   law, 103-112
   medicaid/medi-cal, 94-101
   mothers, 13-16
   paternity, 31-44
   resources, 24-30
   responsibility, 118-122
   school, 113-117
   welfare (AFDC), 71-87
Visitation:
   unwed fathers rights, 19
   court ordered, 65
   legal assistance, 108-109
Welfare (see AFDC)
Women, Infants, and Children (WIC):
   definition, 91
   eligibility, 91-92
Young unwed mothers:
   legal, 103-111
   needs, 13-16
   paternity, 34-35, 38-40
   welfare, 73, 75-76, 78-80

'ON THE FRONTLINE' LEARNING SERIES

Bold New Resources for **UNWED TEEN PARENTS**

Suggested for:
- Teen parent programs
- Home economics
- Libraries
- Family courts
- Hospitals
- Social services
- Crisis intervention

SUPPORT NETWORK

Triangle labels: TEEN MOTHER (Social Services, Health & Child Care) — FATHER (School, Job Programs, Counseling) — CHILD — LAW

FREE "Paternity I.Q. & Resource Kit"
An evaluative tool for your teen parents.

'ON THE FRONTLINE' Learning Series
offers you a complete learning program:

- Text for teen parents
- Student Activity Workbook
- Teachers: Resource/Crisis Intervention Guide
- Teen Parents Supportive Tapes
- Grandparents Active Outreach Tapes

ALL MATERIALS PREPARED WITH THE HELP OF OUR TEENAGE PARENTS ADVISORY COMMITTEE.

For information write:
ADVOCACY CENTER FOR CHILD SUPPORT, INC. • P.O. Box 276
Yorklyn, Delaware 19736 • (302) 239-7203